Child Sex Trafficking in Canada

And how to stop it

"When I served as a Member of the Canadian Parliament, I quickly learned I could not go it alone. In order to get anything meaningful done, a legislator had to ally herself or himself with a certain cadre of people. Those people had to be learned, experienced, reliable, relevant, and—most of all—truly committed to the welfare of their communities. Cathy Peters has earned the right to the attention not only of legislators but also to you as a reader. She has put in thousands of hours of her time as a volunteer to make life better for hapless, trafficked human beings. Her many victories, humbly evident from her well-written, carefully referenced book, light the way to a better Canada and a better world. We would have better legislators tomorrow if we had more people like Cathy Peters today."
—John Weston, Strategic Advisor, former MP, B.C.

"Cathy Peters is a passionate and tireless advocate for trafficking victims and those trapped in the commercial sex industry. Her harrowing book uncovers the sombre reality of exploitation, leaving the reader encouraged to fight against injustice and demand an equitable existence for all."
—Andrea Heinz, Exited Sex Seller, Alberta

"Cathy Peters is a champion of the anti-trafficking community; working tirelessly to bring awareness to a topic most prefer to pretend doesn't exist. Cathy has now punctuated her vocal efforts with this written exemplification on the grievous issue of human trafficking that is occurring right under their noses. Part academic research, part real-life story, *Child Sex Trafficking in Canada and How To Stop It* cleverly grabs a hold of both the reader's heart and their intellect and leaves them with no option but to act."
—Alexandra Stevenson, Writer, Academic, Trafficked Survivor

"At the Arthur V. Mauro Institute for Peace and Justice, where I studied for my Ph.D. in Peace and Conflict Studies, world-class scholars taught us the impact of storytelling in peace building. There, and through a thirty-five-year career in public safety and law enforcement, I have learned the importance of public discourse in making positive change. True change can only occur when the momentum of public opinion moves in the right direction. It was a significant finding in my dissertation research on counter-sex trafficking, and is a major theme of Cathy Peters' new book, *Child Sex Trafficking in Canada and How To Stop It*.

Weaving in the personal stories of sex trafficking survivors, Cathy Peters describes her journey, discovering the injustices and extent of sex trafficking in Canada. The book documents her journey, raising awareness and opinion around sex trafficking in Canada. The important theme that stands out to me in this work is a demonstration of how one person can make a difference and inspire others to do the same."
—Bob Chrismas, Ph.D., Law Enforcement Officer, Manitoba

"As a tireless victim's advocate, Cathy Peters has given voice to the thousands of vulnerable Canadian children who have fallen prey to the inherently evil practice of human trafficking sexual exploitation. *Child Sex Trafficking in Canada and How To Stop It* highlights the very real plight of young Canadians, who are lured or otherwise enticed into sex trafficking rings and then find it difficult, if not impossible, to escape from their enslavement. Cathy also proposes a number of "fixes" that would give law enforcement and social service agencies better tools with which to bring this crisis out of the shadows and interdict the criminal gangs that prey upon our youth. Kudos to Cathy Peters on this important work."
—Hon. Ed Fast, PC, QC, Member of Parliament, B.C.

"Cathy's book is a must-read. It will disturb you. It will make you angry and sad. But hopefully it will encourage you to do something. You can. And this book tells you how. Everyone needs to recognize that sex trafficking exists in Canada and collectively we should do everything in our power to prevent and educate our girls and boys on how they can avoid becoming a statistic. And to the men, please recognize that you have a choice to be part of the solution. Or part of the problem. Choose the former. Let's all help Cathy stop this scourge."
—Jane Thornthwaite, former Provincial MLA, B.C.

"Cathy's book *Child Sex Trafficking in Canada and How To Stop It* is a must-read for all people, especially parents. It's a heart wrenching study of prostitution in Canada by a most passionate and dedicated person that cares deeply about eradicating child sex trafficking in the world beginning here in our country. In 2018 I invited Cathy to attend the AKBLG regional conference that was hosted by my Fernie Council. She conducted a session, spoke to the crowd at the end of the conference and made visits to the schools and police headquarters.

Her book provides much information on resources and stories on survivors that will impact your heart and bring tears to your eyes. My wish is that this book could be found in all libraries and schools so it could become a learning tool for not only parents but all educators. Thank you, Cathy Peters, for your love of humanity and for making a difference by your continued perseverance in this crisis."
—Mary Giuliano, Writer, Former Councillor & Mayor, Fernie, B.C.

"It is great to see Cathy so inspired by the issue and how she continues to advocate and spotlight the cause."
—Janet Campbell, President & CEO, Joy Smith Foundation
—Joy Smith, B.Ed. M.Ed. OM, Founder of the Joy Smith Foundation

Child Sex Trafficking in Canada
and How To Stop It

Cathy Peters

You know that the beginning is the most important part of any work, especially in the case of a young and tender thing; for that is the time at which the character is being formed and the desired impression is more readily taken... shall we just carelessly allow children to hear any casual tales which may be devised by casual persons, and to receive into their minds ideas for the most part the very opposite of those which we should wish them to have when they are grown up?

We cannot... Anything received into the mind at that age is likely to become indelible and unalterable; and therefore, is it not important that the tales which the young first hear should be models of virtuous thoughts...

Then will our youth dwell in a land of health, amid fair sights and sounds, and receive the good in everything; and beauty, the effluence of fair works, shall flow into the eye and ear, like a health-giving breeze from a purer region, and insensibly draw the soul from the earliest years into likeness and sympathy with the beauty of reason.

There can be no nobler training than that.

The Republic
Plato, 360 B.C.E.

This book is dedicated to:
- Karen, a survivor who had the courage to speak up.
- Joy Smith, former Manitoba MP and Canada's authority on human trafficking.
- Law enforcement and first responders, for saving lives.
- To my husband, who said I had to write this book.
- To my family, because they could represent any family in Canada.
- To Indigenous women I have met who tell me to keep going.
- To men and boys who want to stop the exploitation and who cherish the women and girls in their lives, and who do not exploit. You are the ones who can speak up and stop this crime.

Thank you to:
- Kelly Arnold, who told me this book was needed.
- Brian McConaghy, formerly with the RCMP, for his advice and encouragement.
- Jane Thornthwaite, former BC MLA (North Vancouver) who supported my work.
- John Weston, former BC MP (West Vancouver-Sunshine Coast-Sea to Sky Country) for his advice and support.
- To the many mayors, city councillors and regional district directors in British Columbia, who support my advocacy.

Contents

Foreword

When I met Cathy Peters, I was immediately impressed by her passion and the knowledge she possessed on human trafficking. Having been a social worker for over thirty-five years I recognized the impact that trafficking, prostitution, pornography and the sexualization of our youth are having on our society.

Cathy's book is an immersive study into the dark world of trafficking for prostitution in Canada. Its reach is universal as trafficking is an escalating problem worldwide. *Child Sex Trafficking in Canada and How To Stop It* is a primer to educate and motivate parents, educators, policy makers, police and health professionals to put an end to this scourge. Unbridled pornography and the risk of trafficking rob our children of their youth and damages children, youth and women.

As a social worker I have witnessed the horrible outcomes of sexual exploitation and abuse, so I especially appreciate the resources for getting help for victims which are detailed throughout the book and highlighted in the appendices.

I trust that this book will surprise you and at times shock you. I know it will ignite your desire to join Cathy's goal of a "prostitution- and trafficking-free world."

—Dr. Pam Chapman, DRS, LCSW, CTRS
Social Worker, USA

Preface

"Be Amazing!
Stop Sexual Exploitation."

CATHY PETERS

This is a book that should never have had to be written. But here we are. Society and culture have come to a point where the most vulnerable are not being protected. Today's youth, children, the vulnerable and marginalized are at a huge risk of early sexualization and sexual predation. They are aggressively targeted for sexual exploitation yet unaware of the insidious, coercive and manipulative tactics of the sex industry. As a society we have a moral obligation to address this exploitation immediately, resolutely and robustly. If we do not do so, the harm caused to future generations will be incalculable.

This book describes the progression of my experience learning about the sexual exploitation of children in Canada, concluding with specific strategies on how we can stop it. Each chapter peels back a deeper level of the issue.

The term "child sex trafficking" covers all victims under age eighteen; this includes young children, older children, adolescents, and older teenagers. Throughout this book when I use the term "child" or "youth" I am referring to a victim within any of these age groups.

Please help me stop this scourge. While this issue has taken decades for me to understand, hopefully this book will shorten the process for the reader. Anyone and everyone can make a difference. And we must.

My awareness of sexual exploitation began over forty years ago teaching in an inner-city high school. This book represents my journey over these years with the last nine years in full-time work raising awareness for politicians, police and the public. Hundreds of people have shared with me about their past sexual trauma. I have documented my presentations, outcomes, letters, responses, stories, emails, conversations, disclosures, and testimonies in order to understand the trends of exploitation in British Columbia. This book is a summary of what I have learned from survivors, families, parents, law enforcement, health providers, frontline stakeholders, Indigenous leaders, educators, and community leaders. The stories of survivors that are included are stated as they were told to me or found online.

Each chapter contains endnotes with references, and I have included an extensive list of resources and research notes at the end of this book. Please also visit my website at beamazingcampaign.org to learn more.

Prologue

The Be Amazing Campaign was launched on International Women's Day—March 8, 2020—accompanied by a simple brochure and website, beamazingcampaign.org. This information was sent to every Canadian Member of Parliament, senator, premier, and attorney general in Canada and then to every politician in British Columbia at the civic, provincial and federal levels. I initiated public presentations on the issue in 2014, and since the campaign was launched three years ago I have given hundreds more. My goal is to raise awareness about the issue of human sex trafficking, sexual exploitation, and child sex trafficking. Presentations are made to politicians, police and the public, and more lately to police boards, school boards, frontline service providers, Indigenous groups, church groups and service clubs such as Rotary, Zonta International, University Women's Club, and Probus. There is a grassroots movement growing that wants to end sexual exploitation.

Human sex trafficking and sexual exploitation is a fast-growing crime worldwide (Chapter 27). It is a lucrative crime targeting youth, children, and the vulnerable.[1] Today's slavery has low costs and huge profits and a trafficker can make hundreds of thousands of dollars per victim per year.[2] Sex buyers[3] in Canada are invisible but drive the sex industry with their demand for commercially paid sex.

Most troubling is that the average age of entry into prostitution is getting younger and younger. There has been a dramatic increase in child exploitation along with the production and consumption of child pornography.[4] Unregulated technology has increased the demand for commercially paid sex with minors.[5]

The reason for this book is that the public in Canada is only marginally aware of the issue. Women, youth, children, and the vulnerable will become potential victims unless we all do something to stop it.

Since 2014, I have made over 600 individual presentations to over 20,000 people, not including those watched online. What is most encouraging is to have received endorsement from law enforcement. It is an honour to have received fourteen Challenge Coins from B.C. detachments: Abbotsford, Victoria, Delta, New Westminster, two from Vancouver Police Department, Kitimat, North Vancouver, Coquitlam, Richmond, Surrey and Chilliwack RCMP detachments, RCMP HQ Counter Exploitation Unit, and Federal Corrections.

My work has been introduced several times in the B.C. Legislature and I have presented to three Federal Justice Committees on Human Trafficking. A highlight was being a keynote speaker to Missing and Murdered Indigenous Women and Girls gatherings, presenting to various Indigenous groups, and providing a booth at the Assembly of First Nations three-day conference in Vancouver in 2022 where I met many Indigenous leaders.

In 2022, I presented at the Global Summit "Connecting to Protect: Addressing the Harms of Porn on Youth from a Public Health Perspective" hosted by the University of Calgary, and I also presented in an RCMP human trafficking webinar for law enforcement across Canada. I was previously nominated for an Order of British Columbia award and the Carol Matusicky Distinguished Service to Families Award, and in June 2022 I was awarded the Queen's Platinum Jubilee Medal for my advocacy work.

Included below are the articles from the Universal Declaration of Human Rights from the United Nations that underline the importance of freedom and human rights that belong to every human being. Human trafficking for the purpose of prostitution is a clear contradiction to these articles. Also included is the definition for human trafficking from the Palermo Protocol and specific sections from the Canadian Charter of Rights that relate to this crime.

Established in 1948, it enshrines the rights and freedoms of all human beings. Below are the specific articles from the declaration that relate to the crime of sexual exploitation. These articles are accepted globally as the best and highest standard for humanity to attain. As you read this book, it is critical to remember these basic principles of human rights: "Peace, dignity and equality on a healthy planet."

Universal Declaration of Human Rights[6]

Article 1: All human beings are born free and equal in dignity and rights.

Article 2: Everyone is entitled to all the rights and freedoms set forth in this Declaration, without distinction of any kind, such as race, colour, sex, language, religion, political or other opinion, national or social origin, property, birth, or other status.

Article 3: Everyone has the right to life, liberty and security of person.

Article 4: No one shall be held in slavery or servitude; slavery and the slave trade shall be prohibited in all their forms.

Article 5: No one shall be subjected to torture or to cruel, inhuman or degrading treatment or punishment.

Article 6: Everyone has the right to recognition everywhere as a person before the law.

Definition of Human Trafficking

The recruitment, transportation, transfer, harbouring or receipt of persons by means of threat, force, coercion, abduction, fraud, or deception. The abuse of power of a position of vulnerability, giving or receiving payment or benefits to have control over another person for the purpose of exploitation. Exploitation can be prostitution, sexual exploitation, forced labour or services, slavery or practices similar to slavery, servitude, or removal of organs.

Palermo Protocol: 2000[7]
United Nations Human Rights

Ratified by Canada May 2002: A formalization of Canada's commitment to end and prevent human trafficking and smuggling.

Canadian Charter of Rights and Freedoms
Section 2: Fundamental Freedoms

Everyone has the following fundamental freedoms:
  A. Freedom of conscience and religion,
  B. Freedom of thought, belief, opinion and expression including freedom of the press and other media of communication,
  C. Freedom of peaceful assembly,
  D. Freedom of association.

Section 7: Legal Rights

Everyone has the right to life, liberty and security of the person and the right not to be deprived thereof except in accordance with the principles of fundamental justice.

Endnotes

1. "New data shows increase in reports of sexual abuse in schools." Julie Ireton, CBC News, November 2, 2022.
2. "Invisible Chains" by Benjamin Perrin, 2010 Viking Canada, page 111. His source was from "Organized Crime and Domestic Trafficking in Persons in Canada." These numbers were from 2008, but are much higher now.
3. A "buyer" is a person—male or female, but typically male—who purchases, or is attempting to purchase, another person for a sex act. A buyer is often called a "john" or a "trick" when discussed in the context of commercial sex.
4. Press Release from Canadian Centre for the Protection of Children: Amanda Todd; statement: "Justice for Todd family, more work ahead to keep children safe online." August 7, 2022.
   Media relations: 1-204-560-0723.
5. Press Release from Canadian Centre for the Protection of Children: "Cybertip.ca marks 20 years of reducing online victimization of a child." September 26, 2022.
6. Universal Declaration of Human Rights, 1948. www.un.org
7. Palermo Protocol, United Nations Human Rights, "Protocol to Prevent, Suppress and Punish Trafficking in Person Especially Women and Children" supplementing the United Nations Convention against Transnational Crime, November 15, 2000 by General Assembly Resolution 55/25. ohchr.org

The Palermo Protocol has a broad scope definition, according to Valiant Richey, Special Advisor to the OSCE (the Organization for Security and Co-operation in Europe which comprises 57 countries and 1 billion people). It is the primary document addressing human trafficking. 177 countries, including Canada, have signed this protocol. As a result, most countries in the world have developed human trafficking statutes. The definition outlines every aspect of the crime of trafficking, so that anyone involved with any part of the activity, is in fact trafficking. The driver, the recruiter, the person who provides housing, whomever writes the ads—every action is trafficking. Valiant also points out that "prostitution" is the word used in International Law, not the term "sex work." The concern is that sex work would be confused with labour exploitation. Sexual exploitation is dramatically different from labour exploitation. Please view Valiant's presentations online; a list is provided in Chapter 27 endnotes.

ABBREVIATIONS

ACE   Adverse Childhood Experiences
C3P   Canadian Centre for the Protection of Children (Canada)
CCTEHT   Canadian Centre to End Human Trafficking (Canada)
CSAM   Child Sex Abuse Material
CST   Child Sex Trafficking
DMST   Domestic Minor Sex Trafficking
ISTAC   International Survivors of Trafficking Advisory Council
MATH   Mothers Against Trafficking Humans
MMIWG   Missing and Murdered Indigenous Women and Girls
NCECC   National Child Exploitation Crime Centre (RCMP)
NCMEC   National Center for Missing and Exploited Children (USA)
NCOSE   National Center on Sexual Exploitation (USA)
NHTEC   National Human Trafficking Education Centre (Canada)
OCTIP   Office to Combat Trafficking in Persons (British Columbia)
OSCE   Organization for Security and Cooperation in Europe. The OSCE has 57
           participating States that span the globe encompassing three continents:
           North America, Europe, and Asia and more than a billion people.
PCEPA   Protection of Communities and Exploited Persons Act (Canada)
PTSD   Post Traumatic Stress Disorder
SANE   Sexual Assault Nurse Examiners
SEE   Sexual Exploitation Education
TIP   Report Trafficking In Persons Report (US State Department)

Warning: The contents of this book may be shocking. It addresses the topic of human sex trafficking, sexual exploitation, and child sex trafficking.

CHAPTER 1

Karen

"A pimp is the guy who sells women and girls the dream but delivers the nightmare."

MEGAN WALKER, FORMER EXECUTIVE DIRECTOR OF
LONDON'S ABUSED WOMEN'S CENTRE, ONTARIO

In the past nine years of public presentations there have been hundreds of survivors who have spoken to me. Two women stood out. Meeting them and hearing their stories are the reason for my advocacy work and for this book.

Karen* was trafficked as a very young girl at eleven years of age, and Sarah* (Chapter 2) was trafficked at twenty-nine years of age. Sex trafficking has a continuum of ages from very young children to thirty years of age. The chief vulnerability is being female.

Volunteering for the Joy Smith Foundation, I met Karen, a trafficked survivor. This meeting changed my life. Joy Smith asked me to take care of Karen for three days because Karen had agreed to go public with her story. She was presenting at a Joy Smith Foundation fundraiser for human trafficking victims and speaking on Winnipeg Radio and CBC Radio. This is a risky thing to do for survivors. Traffickers could

*Names have been changed to protect privacy.

1

potentially kill any girl that speaks out against them. One reason she was willing to speak up was because her trafficker was dead.

Karen's story is not dissimilar from what many trafficked individuals experience in Canada. Karen, a white girl, grew up in Toronto in a home with her mother and father and five siblings younger than her. Karen was smart, got straight As in school, was a track star and played the flute. But her father began to drink, and since her mother was not able to hold the family together on her own, the family fell apart. Each of the six children were put into foster care homes.

In Karen's foster care home, the foster father sexually assaulted her. She knew it was wrong and ran from home. Within two hours on the streets in Toronto, an older gentleman who said he would take care of her picked her up. He said he had a house full of girls just like her. That night she was introduced to alcohol and cocaine and started sexually servicing ten to twenty men a night, seven days a week for the next ten years.

Joy, who has made thousands of interventions, helped Karen get out of the sex trade; first with detox, then with schooling. I met Karen when she was part way through her schooling.

During the CBC Radio interview, everyone in the studio listened to Karen tell her story. I broke down and wept. How and why would an eleven-year-old in Canada be bought and sold for sex? It was shocking. How could this possibly happen in Canada, renown for a strong history of human rights with emphasis on gender equality?

In the taxi back to the hotel with Joy, I sat in the back seat with Karen and could not stop crying; reminded of our own daughters who were the same age as her. She was very upset with my outburst and told me everything was fine. I told her it was not fine, that this could not happen in Canada, and that it was going to stop.

I promised her it would stop in British Columbia. It was not credible to promise her anything more than addressing the scourge in my own province. Little did I know at the time that B.C. was the furthest behind all provinces in Canada in addressing this crime. And the province continues to get further and further behind in terms of enforcement of the law and lack of public awareness. Tragically in B.C. we have seen the most troubling cases of a victim (Amanda Todd), a trafficker (Reza Moazami), and a sex buyer (Robert Pickton).

Joy heard my promise, and she still reminds me of it. After the three days with Karen, I was inspired to raise awareness about human sex trafficking with as many people as possible.

CHAPTER 2

Sarah

"Sometimes even to live is an act of courage."

SENECA

A city councillor had met a survivor who wanted to tell her story, and contacted me. Since 2014, I had been sending regular emails to city councils across B.C., so it was not unusual for mayors or city councillors to reach out to me. I was doing in-person presentations around B.C. and was able to meet Sarah* in her town in a coffee shop before she started work. This is her story.

Sarah's childhood trauma started at the age of six when a family friend sexually abused her. She started drinking and smoking by the age of eleven to numb the pain of her childhood trauma. By fourteen, her addiction was in full force, doing drugs along with drinking. By this point she was hanging out with an older crowd, and was raped by a man that she met through a friend.

Even though she was doing well in school, Sarah dropped out and at the age of sixteen was working full time to support herself. She moved out of her parent's house a few times between the ages of fifteen and twenty, and had her own place in her mid-twenties.

*Name has been changed to protect privacy.

At sixteen, before she met her trafficker, she was hanging out with people who were involved in criminal activities. She had become an alcoholic and used drinking to numb her pain.

Her parents were always close to her. In later years, once she got away from that life, her dad said, "Sarah, you lived a double life." Sarah hid many things to protect her parents. Her parents always knew something was not right, but Sarah did her best to keep the good people in her life away from the bad people she hung around. Ultimately this became an exhausting cycle to maintain. Her parents, even though at times found it very hard to support her, never wanted to push her away. The thought of losing her kept them connected.

By the time she was in her twenties, she was once again hanging around older people; some of them involved with criminal life. She met her trafficker at a nightclub. He was a "Romeo pimp" who was very likeable and smart. Romeo pimps or lover boys are human traffickers who try to make victims fall in love with them. Once victims are under their influence, they exploit them, typically into the sex industry.

Sarah thought he was everything she needed. She did not realize at the time that he was learning how to pimp and came from a wealthy pimping family in the city. He was in fact a pimp in training. He was of a different nationality and religion. His family was from another country originally although he was born in Canada. He was the eldest son in his family. His cultural expectations were unfamiliar to Sarah and she was unprepared for his treatment of her.

Sarah met her trafficker in March and by August she was being advertised for sex on Backpage, a classified advertising website similar to Craigslist. The process of being trafficked or pimped out happened very quickly. The turning point incident took place a few weeks after they met and after they had hung out together many times. It took only two hours one night, when she was drugged and gang raped at his house by his friends. He blamed her for what happened. The blaming and manipulation were the start of the control he was gaining over her.

Sarah told me that traffickers try and see how far they can go with a girl. Within one week of meeting a girl they know what they can get away with. Traffickers are sophisticated. The traffickers she met were young and attractive, averaging twenty-two years of age. They made a lot of money from the girls they trafficked. Her trafficker was also involved with organized crime.

The more control he had over her, the more violent he became. His goal was to move to Toronto, but her family was in the west and she was resistant to leave her city. She maintained a good and close relationship with her family, but her trafficker used this against her. At one point Sarah got to the point that she did not care if she lived or died, but when her trafficker threatened to hurt her parents, she could not handle that and was going to protect them.

She was required or encouraged by her trafficker to keep her full-time job, as that showed a way of making money and on paper it made her look good. However, her life was one of constant survival and lying to the people she loved, while pleasing a person who only saw her as a dollar sign.

He told her that no one would want her if she left him. She was not allowed to keep any of the money she made selling herself. Fear was his power tactic. She also knew that he owned a lot of guns. He threatened her repeatedly, revealing a Dr. Jekyll and Mr. Hyde split personality. He would become terrifying, especially when he was drunk. At one point he tried to drown her in the bathtub. She thought she was going to die. Sarah knew about pimping, but never understood the dangerous dynamic. She thought girls chose to be prostituted. Around this time, she was twenty-nine and he was twenty-five.

Along with her full-time day job she was prostituted at night and sold on weekends as an escort. She did not do the less-sophisticated car dates but did incalls and outcalls to homes. She frequently used a friend's apartment. She became street smart, learning to think fast. Her life was volatile and circumstances could change quickly. She told me that the general idea that you can screen dates is ridiculous because it is impossible to know what will happen with a sex buyer. They are completely unpredictable.

Her clients were well-to-do businessmen employed by good companies. She serviced regulars. For these men, she was their outlet to express their fetishes. In the room with these men, she learned to act. She disassociated herself from what was happening to survive. Her sense of reality became twisted.

She had become completely loyal to her trafficker, trained on what to do and say if police arrived. Instinctively she never trusted a sex buyer or john. She lied to them to survive. All the girls she knew were taught to appear happy and friendly, but it was all acting. Otherwise, they were severely beaten and raped by their traffickers.

She was charged out at $200 to $240 an hour—it would be significantly more today. In her first month of working, she was making $10,000 a month plus what she brought in from her full-time job, but her pimp boyfriend kept the money. She became a wreck and developed an ulcer. She slept three to four hours a night and continued to be addicted to alcohol.

She considered the move to Toronto when her trafficker suggested it. She was exhausted lying to her family, but she wanted to protect them. Her traffickers violence escalated to such a point that she knew she was going to die because her lifestyle would kill her, or the alcohol she consumed would poison her. Mostly she feared her trafficker because he was very unstable when he was drunk, which was a lot of the time.

She remembers the night when he said to her, after he beat her up, that the only downfall in life would be "when he puts a bullet in her head." When she begged him to leave and find someone else, his exact words were "Why would I let you leave, when I have already put all this time into you? No, it is not going to happen that way." Sarah was a goldmine, and he was not going to let her go. He had a gun, and she knew he would use it if needed. When he got the idea that she would try to get away, he escalated the violence, beating her even more, confining her in a room.

Her mother once told her, "If you hang out with a snake, you will become a snake." Sarah knew she was becoming a snake, living and learning from the extreme criminal environment she was living in. The shame and worthlessness she felt was overwhelming. Her parents stayed connected and in touch with her. She believes that is what saved her life. They did not know what she was involved in. Now that she is out of "The Life," she has a very good and close relationship with her parents, and they are very supportive of her.

A female police detective helped Sarah initially. Sarah was motivated to get out of The Life when her trafficker threatened to kill her family. The detective helped her get away and Sarah was prepared to charge her trafficker, but he was killed. Once Sarah made the call to her detective, her whole life changed, and she never went back to the condo where she lived. Steps were taken to help her leave the city.

Over time her family started to discover some things she was involved in with her trafficker. They knew he hit her because they saw the bruises. She made up lies to cover up what was going on, but as much as it hurt them to not call police or get involved, they just prayed that by not pushing her away, she could come back to them. Ultimately, she did come back to them. Once Sarah made the call to the police, she made her parents aware of everything and they stayed by her side to support her. That is the one thing they did all through the awful ordeal. It was their connection that convinced her to stay in the city and not leave for Toronto, as much as the trafficker tried to isolate her from her parents.

Sarah offers advice to anyone trapped in this life, "There is a way out and you can heal. Staying with a trafficker only gets worse. But once a person gets away, that person can learn to love again. Good people will come alongside and help, stay and support." This was Sarah's experience.

To recover from her encounter with prostitution, Sarah realized it needed to be a priority to address her addictions. She signed up for a recovery program with help and support. She has now been sober for many years. She has good friends, a college diploma, a good job, and a wonderful family.

Her advice to politicians and police: "Things must be made tougher for the demand side. The buyers need to be stopped and deterred from buying sex. Backpage made it too easy for buyers to find escorts."

She encourages families to stay strong and connected to their children because that made the difference for her. As a young person who experienced sexual trauma, she had low self-esteem and was emotionally broken, making her vulnerable even into her late twenties.

She told me it is important for girls to speak about what is happening to them. They need to share their voice. If a girl feels insecure, she needs to find a positive friend group. Sarah is concerned that social media is a big problem today and it is important for parents to learn about media culture and watch their children's media posts. Communication with children is key. Sarah also believes that pornography fuels the sex industry.

I deeply appreciated the fact that Sarah took time with me to share her experience. Her experience being trafficked as an adult, contrasts with Karen's experience who was underage when she was prostituted. Sarah realized her trafficking experience should have never happened. She made the point to me that anyone can be manipulated, at any age or stage of their lives. Both Karen and Sarah were robbed of their dignity and human rights by their traffickers and by the men that bought them for sex.

In dating violence and abuse there are stages that are similar to the grooming strategies used by traffickers.[1] These are red flags for any relationship and this progression was part of Sarah's experience. Parents need to be aware of significant changes in their children that could be red flags or signs of an unsafe relationship.

Early stages. Beginning with love-bombing, this is a tactic in which a person uses excessive and disproportionate gestures of affection with the goal of manipulation and establishing control over their partner. "Too good to be true" begins the relationship.

Isolation. This is a control tactic and can occur early in the relationship.

Control. There is jealousy, possessiveness, manipulation, stalking and monitoring.

Manipulation. Name calling, unfair pressure and requests, blaming, guilt trips, makes their partner feel crazy.

Mood swings. Threats, sudden anger, hurts the partner or hurts themselves.

Endnotes

1   Survivor Ashley Bendiksen with International Difference Makers is an award-winning activist and motivational speaker who explains about dating violence and abuse. She presented at the 2021 NCOSE (National Center on Sexual Exploitation) Global summit describing the stages of the most common controlling coercive behaviours in dating violence and abuse.

CHAPTER 3

A Letter

"This triangle of truisms, of father, mother and child, cannot be destroyed; it can only destroy those civilizations which disregard it."

G.K. CHESTERSON

Below is a letter I received from a parent in November 2021. It illustrates the seriousness and prevalence of the issue and extent of the crime in Canada. This parent has asked me to share her letter as widely as possible to warn the public and raise awareness.

I am writing to you as a concerned parent and citizen. I would like to bring to your attention an epidemic that, in my observation, has not been adequately addressed within the legal and law enforcement sectors here in Canada. The epidemic I speak of is the prevalence of online predation, luring, grooming, and sexual exploitation of children and youth. These can and do often lead to trafficking and the production of child pornography, among other atrocities. As a family we have experienced the horrors of this firsthand.

My daughter, who was a minor at the time, was groomed and lured online by an adult predator. The predator acquired more than fourteen sexually exploitative videos of our daughter. The predator had committed voyeurism (making, observing, and possession of child pornography (Criminal Code of Canada: 163.1(1) and luring of a minor 172.1(1)). The communication between him and my daughter, through social media, pointed to his intentions of also sexually exploiting her (Criminal Code of Canada: 152), both personally and through distribution of child pornography and prostitution (trafficking). We were able to intervene and sought help just before she was to run away to meet the individual.

During the process of discovering knowledge of the predator, and then seeking out help, we had contacted the RCMP (as well as the County Police in the USA where the individual resided), Cybertip.ca, and other law enforcement agencies that we were directed to. We had pictures of the perpetrator, proof of identity (through my daughter identifying him to us since she saw him through video calls), a full name, birthdate, place of residence, and multiple social media address (usernames), and a detailed file with all the communication between the predator and my daughter. He was easy to track online since he had prior convictions.

This crime went unpunished.

As parents we were faced with the difficult decision of supporting her in healing from this traumatic event and helping her move forward, rather than seeking justice. And yet, it should not have to be a choice between the two. If protocols were changed for investigating predators, then children and youth (and families) would have the space they need to heal from the trauma, while having law enforcement fight for justice on behalf of the family.

Children and youth, because of fear of punishment, or fear of reprisal do not report the majority of incidents of their predation by the predator (Sexual Exploitation over the Internet: A Rapid Review of the Scientific Literature, April 2020, Institute of Health Economics, Maria Ospira, Christa Harstall, and Liz Dennett). I would add that the victim might feel shame or attachment to their abuser (Stockholm Syndrome or trauma bond).

To me, as a mother, it is appalling that these perpetrators, who have severely damaged the life and development of these children and youth, and have caused such intense pain to the families, would get an average of one to three years in prison, if they get convicted at all.

There are approximately 500,000 predators online in a day (Source: Innocent Lives Foundation at the Disrupt Demand: Canada Sexual Exploitation Summit 2021). This is a serious issue and one that needs to be addressed before more children are lost to trafficking, child pornography and the damages of exploitation.

Our daughter was one of the 'lucky ones' who was intercepted in time before more damage was done, and yet the mental health effects of the abuse and trauma are still with her long after the ties to her predator have been cut. She is still vulnerable.

We tried reporting to the social media platforms (Instagram and Facebook) where the predator was contacting our daughter and they did not investigate our reports, which is extremely concerning.

These experiences are not unique to my family. Thousands of families across Canada have been similarly impacted and this issue is escalating.

We were able to seek out the help our daughter needed just before she was to run away to meet the individual. She was able to disentangle from the predator through mental health resources within our community, which we are very grateful for and continue to navigate. We have been part of a parent group where many parents have sadly lost their children.

CHAPTER 4

Teaching

"I cannot emphasize enough the importance of a good teacher."

TEMPLE GRANDIN

Coming from a family of educators, I love teaching. My grandmother taught grades one to eight in a northern Manitoba one-room classroom. My mother taught in a city high school and my father was an award-winning university professor.

In high school my dream was to become a doctor. But at university, I discovered that sciences were not a passion. To help people, particularly youth, there was a more straightforward path to follow that dream. Switching to Home Economics and Education and after graduating in five years, I immediately started teaching

My first job was in a small rural community in British Columbia. Then a move to the Lower Mainland where I taught in a junior high school near the King George Highway. The King George Highway was a 'kiddie stroll' over forty years ago and continues to be today where youth sell their bodies for sex. What I witnessed in that high school then has become the norm in many high schools in the country.

My five years of teaching was challenging during the early 1980s. In the rural school I had nine classes to prepare for grades eight to twelve, plus coaching. It was a farming community, and my students came from hard-working homes. The students sat long hours on the school bus to and from school yet were involved with a lot of extra-curricular activities. The school had committed experienced teachers and very few students fell through the cracks.

The work hours were long but I saw the advantage of strong sports teams, clubs, industrial arts, home economics, art and music programs offered by the school. The students worked hard and were challenged. Student council was strong and active. Indigenous students shared their culture proudly at the school. The school functioned well for the students and the community was supportive of the school.

Moving to the Lower Mainland was a shock. My teaching day was much shorter, and there were only two class preparations instead of nine. The school was not the centre of the community in the same way it was in my previous rural school. The students were tough, hardened, disrespectful, and many came from very difficult home situations. Numerous students lived with Adverse Childhood Experiences[1] or ACEs (a term I learned forty years later) or unaddressed trauma.

I taught Foods and Nutrition in a large room with six kitchens and learned to teach while never turning my back on my students. Watching carefully otherwise students would turn ovens on, steal food from my cupboards, and cause general mischief. I had to be always hyper-vigilant and super-organized. Each lesson had to be focused and engaging. These were the important teaching skills to learn during those years. In a reversal of roles, my students taught me.

Teaching Foods and Nutrition had an advantage over teaching other subject classes because the students got to eat what they cooked. For many students it was an important meal of the day. Some were in foster care, some had drug issues, and a few were in youth probation. To inspire my students and give them hope, was my goal.

These years were particularly rewarding. Watching the maturing of young people making wise decisions was remarkable. Many students overcame tremendous adversity in their lives. It was a wonderful experience to watch students achieve success whether it was to perfect an apple strudel or cook a meal for guests we invited to class. Coaching sports teams was extremely rewarding; seeing students give everything in terms of discipline and practice to win a game or championship. The sense of pride of achievement by these students made teaching a life-fulfilling experience for me. It was preparation for what I would dedicate my efforts to many years later.

Endnotes

1   "ACEs and Toxic Stress: Frequently Asked Questions" Center on the Developing Child, Harvard University. developingchild.harvard.edu

CHAPTER 5

Cambodia

"You may choose to look
the other way, but you can never say
again that you did not know."

WILLIAM WILBERFORCE

*British politician and philanthropist who from 1787 led the parliamentary campaign
to abolish the slave trade and to abolish slavery itself in British overseas possessions.*

Brian McConaghy was a former RCMP forensics expert. He had the horrendous job of identifying the body parts of prostituted women on the Robert Pickton farm in Port Coquitlam. Robert Pickton was a notorious serial killer who targeted vulnerable women for his sexual exploits and then disposed of their remains by feeding their body parts to his pigs or by grinding them up at a meat rendering plant. He is considered one of the worst and most savage killers in Canadian legal history. Pickton was a sex buyer who bought prostituted women in Vancouver's Downtown Eastside; an area of neglected hotels, a burgeoning drug trade and street-level survival prostitution. Many of his victims were of Indigenous heritage. Pickton's egregious crimes shocked the world as the details of his brutality were revealed.

Brian is also recognized as an expert investigator of child sex tourism. He successfully probed the cases of Donald Bakker[1] and Christopher Neil;[2] Canadians who were pedophiles that preyed on very young

South Asian children. On hearing a presentation by Brian thirty years ago, we were appalled to learn that Canadian businessmen travelled overseas to have sex with children.

After working for the RCMP, Brian went on to establish the NGO, Ratanak International,[3] whose efforts focus on the war-scarred country of Cambodia. For decades Brian has worked tirelessly to raise awareness about sexual exploitation with the Cambodian government, to help rebuild the country and to protect women and children from a rampant, undeterred sex industry. His well-trained staff bring freedom and hope to the lives of women and girls who have been trapped in the sex industry. The vision and mission of Ratanak is to see transformation in Cambodia by empowering people experiencing exploitation and addressing the systems that exploit them. Since first hearing of Brian's work, we have supported Ratanak International in their work to rescue, rehabilitate and restore young Cambodian women and girls, including a growing number of boys.

Brian McConaghy understands the ploys of the sex industry globally. He also understands it is a growing problem in Canada. Brian encouraged Manitoba Member of Parliament Joy Smith to make changes in the federal law so that Canada would discourage the development of the sex industry. Brian speaks nationally and internationally on the plight of the most vulnerable and marginalized.

Following is Brian's compelling presentation to the Standing Committee of the Justice and Human Rights hearings of Canada on the introduction of a new law in Canada, PCEPA, the Protection of Communities and Exploited Persons Act, July 10, 2014 (Evidence - JUST (41-2) No. 43). I have included his presentation because he graphically summarizes the seriousness of the issue in Canada from the perspective of a global expert on this crime.

Mr. Chair, ladies and gentlemen, thank you for the opportunity to speak. My name is Brian McConaghy and I come to the issue of prostitution with twenty-two years of experience in the RCMP and twenty-four years directing Ratanak International, a charity that assists Cambodian youth to recover from the abuses of the sex trade. While in the RCMP, I was assigned files that involved both domestic and international prostitution. So grave were the abuses visited upon both women and children in these files that I was compelled to leave the RCMP in order to serve such victims full time. It is now my challenge and privilege to do so. I continue to assist Canadian law enforcement in international investigations associated with prostituted children and youth.

Bill C-36 seeks to address some very complex issues and I would like to commend the government for its efforts to identify those prostituted as victims rather than criminals. I would also support criminalizing those who purchase and benefit from the sale of Canadian women.

I need to begin by stating that I judge human trafficking and prostitution as inseparable and simply different elements of the same criminal activity, which exploits vulnerable women and youth. The separation of these elements I view to be largely academic.

I should also indicate that while there are clear distinctions in law regarding the treatment of minors and adults in prostitution, I view this as a seamless continuum of abuse that runs from the prostituted child, who by virtue of age is deemed incompetent to consent, and progresses into the abused adult, who by virtue of conditioning, addiction, and trauma is frequently rendered equally incapable of informed and considered consent. Thus, the issues of minors, while not directly associated with the Bedford ruling, are clearly material to these deliberations.

I would like to address several contextual issues to which Bill C-36 applies.

First is harm reduction and legalization. Those "harm reduction" principles frequently verbalized by those seeking to legalize the prostitution industry are, I believe, misguided. I have not seen any convincing evidence to indicate that women in prostitution will be safer if regulated. If anything, legalizing the sex trade will, if we consider Germany and the Netherlands, increase the size and scope of the trade, leading to more human trafficking, more involvement of organized crime, more prostitution and de facto more violence.

It is in my opinion foolish to presume that the introduction of regulations to an industry such as prostitution will lead to compliance and cooperation. This is particularly true given the number of minors manipulated into the trade and the number of women struggling with addiction, mental illness, and financial vulnerabilities who are not necessarily in control of their own lives. If prostitution is legalized, I would anticipate that many of these women will fall through the regulatory cracks.

I do not believe that legalization and regulation would have protected the women Willie Pickton picked up who ended up dismembered in my RCMP freezers for forensic analysis. What we learn from the Pickton file and the analysis of their body parts, indicates that Pickton was only the last in a long line of predators who had over the years subjected these women to traumatic abuse and injury.

Let us be under no illusion as to the brutality of this industry. Defenceless Canadian citizens are being routinely subjected to great harm in prostitution, and their vulnerabilities are being exploited to the full. I have watched too many evidence videos involving profound violence, degradation and abuse. I have listened to women and children as they have pleaded for the torture; I use the term advisedly, to stop. I would not wish such videos on any of you. In this context, the issue of consent looms large. Tragically, some of the victims consent to such bodily harm and physical injury at the hands of johns simply because they are so desperate for their next drug fix. Let us not presume that what passes, as consent is actually full informed consent free of duress.

It is this peripheral violence that the practices of harm reduction would seek to address. However, harm reduction in the context of legalized prostitution would do nothing to address the violence inherent in the central sexual activity of prostitution. It is my belief that such central activity, which is the career of prostitution, does in fact represent violence against women. Harm reduction practices will not protect women from violence if the job, itself, represents violence.

The purchasing of women's consent by males and subjecting them to thousands of paid rapes does violence to their bodies and is profoundly destructive to the psyche. Young women exiting out of enforced prostitution frequently feel suicidal and they do attempt suicide.

It is interesting to me that I have never encountered a young woman in a transitional program who has attempted suicide because of her memories of beatings, being held at gunpoint, or being stabbed. Invariably, the source of their distress is a profound sense of worthlessness resulting from the repeated sexual assaults that are central to the job, along with constant dehumanizing verbal abuse that undermines their self-esteem and shakes their identity to the core; this is the central violence of prostitution.

If then, violence is central to the life of prostitution, the only clear way to reduce violence is to reduce the size of the trade. Experimentation in other nations teaches us that legalization will not reduce the harm but rather, by growing the trade, will increase it. In addition, I believe we are naïve if we assume the creation of a legalized Canadian industry of sex abuse would be unnoticed by the very large source of demand south of the border. Simple economics will dictate that the demand will be filled with increasingly vulnerable 'product', which will be found within Canadian society. Providing such a market is potentially catastrophic.

On the issue of choice, it is my belief that the law needs to target those who clearly have choice in regard to such harm. Those vulnerable women, both minors and adults, the majority of whom have experienced abuse as children, were frequently drug-addicted, manipulated, and extremely vulnerable, do not have that choice.

However, those with money, careers, and a reputation to maintain; those who kiss their kids goodnight, say goodbye to their wives, get in the car, drive downtown, and choose to abuse a vulnerable woman or girl, these are the ones our laws clearly need to be directed towards. Bill C-36 does this, for *the first time, targeting johns and those who would pimp. This represents a major step forward.*

As one who has spent far too much time picking through the dismembered body parts of prostituted women, analyzing the nature and circumstances of their brutal deaths; as one who knows first-hand how many years it takes to rehabilitate systematically abused youth, and as one who devoted his life to the recovery of such victims, allow me to assure you this is not an industry of choice for the vast majority of those prostituted. It is neither lucrative nor empowering for them. It is fundamentally coercive and manipulative. It is abusive, violent, and destructive on every level, and it is deadly. Prostitution and its end game of psychological damage, physical injury and even death should never be celebrated or legalized, only condemned.

One of the key indicators of a mature democracy is its ability to look past the superficial and move to create legislation that protects the most vulnerable and abused, irrespective of their circumstances or standing in society. In creating this legislation, Canada has moved to protect victimized women, who are frequently not recognized as victims by virtue of their circumstance and appearance. This, in conjunction with a concerted effort to prosecute those who would victimize them and capitalize on their misfortunes, is both honourable and appropriate.

Endnotes

1 "Pedophile sex tourist gets ten years for assaults" by Petti Fong, Globe and Mail, June 3, 2005.
2 "Swirl Face pedophile Christopher Neil sentenced to five-and-a-half years in prison" CBC News British Columbia, June 1, 2016.
3 Ratanak International. ratanak.org

CHAPTER 6

Joy Smith

"Education is our greatest weapon."

JOY SMITH

Former Manitoba Member of Parliament and founder of the Joy Smith Foundation

During the years that we got to know Brian, he became close friends with Manitoba Member of Parliament Joy Smith. Coincidentally, our son began working for Joy in her Ottawa MP office as a communications advisor. He informed us of Joy's timely work, as she was assisting girls out of the sex industry and exposing the crime of human trafficking in Canada. I was invited to Ottawa and to Winnipeg to volunteer with Joy and her team.

To watch Joy in action was inspiring to say the least. Her passion to expose the sex industry for what it is—manipulative, coercive, brutal, inhumane, and deadly—was relentless. Joy has since left politics and works with her NGO, the Joy Smith Foundation.[1] Her daughter, Janet, is the executive director. They have recently launched the National Human Trafficking Education Centre, which is an invaluable educational resource for anyone to access and use. There are multiple modules covering every topic related to human trafficking. Since she has worked with thousands of survivors, they have taught her what human trafficking looks like, how it works, and how to stop it.

Joy and her team are available to speak and present anywhere in Canada and she is well known internationally. Joy recognizes the serious urgency for addressing this crime. Canadian laws in human trafficking are quite new and she was instrumental in introducing them in Canada. She introduced two private member's bills that became law: Bill C-268 with its mandatory minimum sentencing for anyone trafficking youth eighteen years and younger, and Bill C-310, the law that extends into other countries to bring perpetrators back to Canada to receive justice. In 2014, she was involved in endorsing the PCEPA law: The Protection of Communities and Exploited Persons Act (Appendix A). She is adamant that these laws need to be upheld, enforced and strengthened consistently across Canada.[2]

Joy has produced DVD documentaries that are useful for training purposes. Paul Boge interviewed her for her book, *The True Story About Human Trafficking in Canada* (Appendix G: Resources). It is a riveting story about Abby Summers, a young teen who was lured into the sex industry. The story is fictional but is a compilation of the stories and lives that Joy has experienced across Canada. The book is a compelling realistic read about human trafficking.

It was by watching Joy present that I learned about the crime. Here is a summary of the main points from her presentations:

Where does human trafficking occur?
- Human trafficking happens everywhere.
- No community is immune and 90% of the problem is domestic (Canadians).
- There is a lot of trafficking between Canada and the USA. Source: NCECC (National Child Exploitation Crime Centre).

Who is the trafficker?

- A predator can be male, female, adults, youth, trusted friends, family, affluent or poor, gang members, or upstanding community members.
- Local citizens or international criminals.
- Traffickers make hundreds of thousands of dollars per victim, so are highly motivated.
- It is a low risk, highly lucrative crime.

Who is at risk to be trafficked?

- The majority are young girls ages twelve to fourteen. Some boys are targeted.
- The ages are getting younger.
- Children are easily influenced and intimidated.
- There is a high demand for children.
- Exploiting children rakes in the highest profit.
- There is a specific market for extremely vulnerable Indigenous women and girls.
- There has been a significant increase in trafficking boys since the beginning of the COVID-19 pandemic.

How does the trafficker groom or lure a victim?

- Traffickers are highly skilled at targeting vulnerable youth.
- Traffickers use befriending or boy-friending tactics and promise gifts to gain trust.
- Traffickers lure through friendship.
- Traffickers are very sophisticated and organized.
- Traffickers will say they love their victims, but this is only temporary.
- They isolate their victims from family and friends.
- Since COVID-19, traffickers have turned to social media to meet and lure victims.

- They will fuel a victim's mistrust of police.
- They withhold necessities of life to control the victim.

How can trafficking be stopped?
- There needs to be a national conversation about the crime.
- There are three pillars to act on: education, collaboration, and healing for the survivors and their families.
- First step is education for parents, teachers, students, the Indigenous, new migrants, police officers and the judiciary.
- The issue in Canada is so big there must be collaboration from everyone.
- Parents, schools, police need to work together.
- We must work with the police as they have become more community minded.
- Healing victim trauma is critical and takes time and resources.

Advice for parents:
- Parents need to keep computers in common spaces.
- No private information should be shared online.
- Photographs or videos should not be shared.
- Selfie Stop is an app that prevents phone users from taking, sending, and uploading nude selfies. Sending nudes is very dangerous and these images cannot be retrieved. 30% of teens have sexted, 40% have received a sext. Of the 30% who have sexted, 46% of those are involved in sextortion.
- Have boundaries and guidelines in the family for internet and phone use. The average age for children to have a smartphone is ten. Teens are spending an average nine hours a day online.

Joy encourages everyone to speak up for those who cannot speak for themselves. Since the COVID-19 pandemic, trafficking has increased exponentially. Joy stresses that it will take a nation to stop this crime.

Joy states that it is very important to maintain the federal law, the Protection of Communities and Exploited Persons Act (PCEPA) and have it consistently enforced across Canada—in Chapter 7 I describe this law in my Justice Committee Presentation; see also Appendix A with preamble to the law. PCEPA targets the sex buyers who are almost exclusively men. To lose PCEPA would be a black mark against Canada and would circumvent the rights of every woman. She talks about Canada's PCEPA law with other countries and leaders. Globally human trafficking is a borderless crime because traffickers move their victims anywhere. There needs to be a call to action in every community and throughout the country.

What you can do: [3]

- Become educated so you recognize the human trafficking indicators.[4]
- Report to police and government officials if you suspect human trafficking is occurring.
- Youth can start a human rights group and learn to protect themselves and each other.
- Talk about the issue.
- Be brave enough to take action. Everything you do to raise awareness helps and could save a life.
- Empower others.

When Joy was member of parliament, USA President Jimmy Carter wrote this powerful letter on May 16, 2014 to Canadian parliamentarians to address the oppression and exploitation of women and children:

"In your efforts to revise your nation's prostitution laws, I encourage you to adopt the highly successful Nordic model. This model targets the pimps and buyers of sex for prosecution instead of the prostitutes, provides long-term funding for exit programs to assist prostituted persons in escaping exploitation and develops a national awareness campaign to promote the equality of women that will expose the violence, inequality and coercion in prostitution. As I noted in my December 27, 2013 op-ed in the Ottawa Citizen, it has been proven that public exposure in a trial and the imposition of a heavy fine or jail time for a few men who are prominent citizens or police officers who were buying or profiting from the sex trade would be extremely effective in helping to eliminate this terrible form of exploitation.

Prostitution is inherently violent, especially towards women and girls, and I support efforts to help those who are trapped in this industry. Your decisive leadership in this matter is critical in order for Canada to take this monumental step toward the preservation of human rights. I hope that you lead your nation towards the protection of prostituted women and girls."

Sincerely,
Jimmy Carter

Endnotes

1   Joy Smith Foundation. joysmithfoundation.com
2   Joy Smith biography at sexualexploitationsummit.ca and look up Current Roles
    and Past roles as Member of Parliament at ourcommons.ca
3   National Strategy to Combat Human Trafficking Annual Report 2020–2021.
    canada.ca/human-trafficking "Trafficking in Persons in Canada, 2020" by Shana
    Conroy and Danielle Sutton, Canadian Centre for Justice and Community Safety
    Statistics. publicsafety.gc.ca

    Canadian Centre to End Human Trafficking.
    canadiancentretoendhumantrafficking.ca
4   The Prevalence of Human Trafficking in Canada. Search for and watch the video
    "The Flesh Trade" by Global News in Calgary, a series by journalist Jill Croteau.
    www2.gov.bc.ca

CHAPTER 7

The Problem

"We need to get to the right question:
Do we want more or less prostitution
in Canada? The evidence is everywhere
in the world, prostitution is unequal,
unhealthy and unfair to women."

JANINE BENEDET, LAW PROFESSOR

Human trafficking is indeed a problem in Canada and here are some examples that occurred in one short week:

February 28, 2022: CTV News Toronto, "Two people face hundreds of charges in Toronto's most prolific and disturbing case of child sexual abuse" by Sean Davidson.

March 1, 2022: CTV News Edmonton, "Human trafficking charges laid after teen girl comes forward."

March 2, 2022: CBC Toronto, "47 Canadians arrested, 6 in Toronto, following New Zealand led probe into horrific online child abuse."

According to the National Center of Missing and Exploited Children's Cyber Tipline in the USA, 2022 was a record-breaking year with twenty-two million reports of suspected child sexual exploitation made in this one year; an increase of 35% in one year. This number is staggering, and still does not represent the whole problem.[1]

Human sex trafficking, sexual exploitation and child sex trafficking are on the rise in Canada as cited by Stats Canada, Federal Public Safety Ministry, Canadian Centre to End Human Trafficking (CCTEHT) and the Trafficking in Persons (TIP) Report 2021 published by the USA State Department. These trends are finally being tracked and documented in Canada. For example, the Canadian Centre to End Trafficking (CCTEHT) just released their first national report (2022) on human trafficking trends.[2]

The Criminal Intelligence Service Canada (CSIC) Strategic Brief (August 2008, Organized Crime and Domestic Trafficking in Persons in Canada) gives a baseline of statistics and the low risk, high reward for traffickers. Typical ages of females trafficked for sexual exploitation by organized crime networks in Canada was twelve to twenty-five years. The average annual profit illicitly earned by organized crime networks from one female trafficked for sexual exploitation in Canada was over $280,000. The average annual profit illicitly earned by organized crime networks from ten females trafficked for sexual exploitation in Canada was over $3,000,000. This baseline today in 2022 has changed. The ages for trafficked victims are younger. The amount of money made per victim is much higher.

Diane Sowden,[3] from Coquitlam B.C., experienced the crime firsthand. In 2013, I met Diane, the founder of Children of the Street Society. Diane worked tirelessly for twenty-five years combatting the growing crime of Child Sexual Exploitation. As a parent she lost her thirteen-year-old daughter to a pimp-trafficker in Vancouver. Hearing Diane's story and the impact on her family is heartbreaking.

Diane's daughter was smart but bored, chose to hang out with older people and started to disappear on weekends. Her daughter was a risk-taker, started using marijuana laced with heroin and became a drug addict.

From this devastatingly traumatic family experience, Diane wanted to help other families to protect their children from sexual exploitation. She started a nationally recognized and successful not-for-profit organization, Children of the Street[4] (now under PLEA) that teaches prevention education from grades four to twelve in B.C. schools, reaching over 25,000 students each year. It is one of the best and most effective prevention education programs for youth in Canada.

What Diane experienced with her own daughter has become more common in today's culture. The internet has made this possible where youth and children are now lured predominantly online. Changes in the criminal code make a big difference, and Diane worked for fourteen years to change the legal age of sexual consent from fourteen to sixteen years. Diane was an Order of Canada recipient in December 2021.[5]

"Prostitution is not the oldest profession in the world, it is the oldest oppression."

JOY SMITH, FORMER MANITOBA MP

Tiana Sharifi was the program director for many years at Children of the Street, then went out on her own to set up SEE—Sexual Exploitation Education.[6] Tiana teaches about the potential harms and dangers on the internet. She has also developed an app for youth to assess risks and dangers of a potential trafficking situation.

As a result of my own work in raising awareness of the problem of child sex trafficking in Canada, the Federal Justice Committee asked me to be a witness at the review of PCEPA, the Protection of Communities and Exploited Persons Act. Below is my presentation to the Standing Committee on Justice and Human Rights: Evidence Number 003, 1st Session 44th Parliament, February 13, 2022. It is an overview of the problem we now have in Canada. The detailed written brief is found in Appendix B.

Thank you, Mr. Chair

I am a former inner city high school teacher raising awareness about human sex trafficking and sexual exploitation for the purpose of prostitution, which is modern day slavery. Here are some statistics: [7]

- *Thirteen is the average age of recruitment, and much younger for Indigenous girls. In the Vancouver area, the target age has dropped to ten to twelve years old. COVID-19 has made this worse.* [8]
- *Traffickers are organized and sophisticated. 90% of the luring, grooming, buying and selling is online on social media platforms (Stats Canada, Cybertip.ca).*
- *54% in the sex trade are Indigenous with 70–90% in urban centres. They are severely over-represented in the sex industry. I told the B.C. Indigenous Chiefs in front of Justice Minister David Lametti that this is the most egregious form of systemic racism in Canada.* [9]
- *82% involved in prostitution had childhood sexual abuse or incest.*
- *72% live with complex PTSD.* [10]
- *95% in prostitution want to leave. It is not a choice or a job.*
- *84% of prostituted persons are pimped or trafficked so organized crime and international crime syndicates are typically involved. Crime follows the money and traffickers make hundreds of thousands of dollars per victim per year.* [11]

My goal is to traffic proof every community in British Columbia and to stop the full decriminalization of prostitution in Canada, by supporting federal law, the Protection of Communities and Exploited Persons Act.

I have been involved with sexual exploitation prevention for over forty years and began raising awareness full-time, for the last eight years, since PCEPA, became federal law.

In 2014, I began presenting to politicians from all three levels of government, the police and the public. I explain PCEPA so that police would enforce it, the public would understand it and be able to report it.

The law has four parts:
- *Targets the demand by targeting the buyer of sex. The traffickers, the facilitators, the buyers of sex are criminalized.*
- *Recognizes the seller of sex as a victim, usually female who is immune from prosecution.*
- *Exit strategies are in place to assist the victim out of the sex trade.*
- *There is robust prevention education so youth, children and the vulnerable are not pulled into the sex industry.*

This law focuses on the source of harm, the buyers of sex and the profiteers. The clear statement from Parliament is that girls and women in Canada are not for sale; they are full human beings, with dignity and human rights.

In the past eight years I have made over 500 presentations to over 20,000 people, not including the presentations that can be viewed online. The turning point was last March when the

Kamloops mass grave was reported. Since then, I have made over 200 presentations to city councils, regional districts, school boards, police boards, schools, frontline service providers, Indigenous groups including MMIWG gatherings in British Columbia. Here are three key points:

- PCEPA is not known or enforced in B.C. Therefore, B.C. is the best province in Canada to buy sex. Organized crime and international crime syndicates are typically involved.
- PCEPA has not had a national rollout campaign, so Canadians have not heard of the law and police are not getting the funding or training to enforce the law.
- The sex industry wants to repeal PCEPA to normalize, commercialize and institutionalize the sex industry in Canada. If this happens, Canada will become a global sex tourism destination and America's brothel. Indigenous women and girls will be first casualties. Canadians would never support this.

Consistent enforcement and the strengthening of PCEPA combined with a robust educational campaign are needed. Without the enforcement of the law, the sex industry will continue to rapidly grow.

The review of PCEPA puts Canada at a tipping point; repealing or weakening the law will have a catastrophic impact on Canada. In conclusion, I do not want anyone on this committee to be under the illusion that the sex industry is safe. It can never be made safe. It is a deadly industry. I have presented with the forensics RCMP officer who picked up and identified the body pieces on the Robert Pickton farm. Trisha Baptie who is presenting in the next hour, is a survivor and was a journalist for two years at the Pickton trial. Please read and understand the

*Robert Pickton case thoroughly; that describes the reality of the
sex industry and how it works.*

I have shared this script with every city council and regional district in
British Columbia to warn them of this growing crime.

Human sex trafficking, sexual exploitation and prostitution all have
common root causes that we need to identify and address, such as
childhood sexual assault, incest, demand for paid sex, and pornography.
These root causes will be discussed throughout this book.

Human trafficking is a rapidly growing crime in the world and in
Canada. There is lack of public awareness. The police and the public
do not have enough knowledge about human trafficking to prevent it.
There are an increasing number of displaced persons and refugees who
will be vulnerable for predation. The internet has no deterrent and is
being used for recruitment locally and globally.

While drugs and weapons can be sold once, a girl can be sold repeatedly.
Years ago, at a BC Public Safety presentation a law enforcement officer
stated that a joint of marijuana would cost $5 to $10, while a trafficker
or pimp could sell half an hour of sex with a fourteen-year-old girl for
$200. And girls are easier to sell. According to what officers have told me
more recently, the profit for selling girls has increased significantly and
traffickers can make hundreds of thousands of dollars a year per victim.

Gangs have diversified in their operations and now use human
trafficking as a fundraiser. It is a low risk, high-income crime for the
gangs. Gangs will operate in the area of exotic dancing and massage
parlours where human trafficking has increased. For young girls, these
gangs become family, often replacing a less-desirable situation at home
or at a youth facility.

The question I am often asked is, "How many victims are there in
Canada each year?" Canada has not kept statistics or data on this, so
law enforcement can only guess. The crime in Canada is clandestine

and hidden although examining Missing Persons Statistics might give a clue of the numbers.

"How many consumers and sex buyers do we have in Canada?" That is the important question because it is the driver for the problem in the first place. Men and boys are the buyers of sex and need to be convinced that women and girls are worthy of respect and have value. We need to teach boys what healthy masculinity and healthy relationships look like (Chapter 29). Whenever I present, boys tell me consistently that they do not want to grow up being rapists and buyers of sex. However, the culture is so toxic that boys are relentlessly targeted by the porn and the sex industry, to become what they hate.

Endnotes

1   CyberTipline 2021 Report, National Center for Missing & Exploited Children. missingkids.org
2   Human Trafficking Trends in Canada, 2019–20, October 14, 2021. The Canadian Centre to End Human Trafficking. canadiancentretoendhumantrafficking.ca
3   "Raising Awareness About Sexual Exploitation—Mother of troubled, drug-addicted former teen shares her story in hopes of educating others" by Meagan Robertson, Squamish Chief, March 7, 2011.
4   Children of the Street. PLEA Community Services Society of BC. childrenofthestreet.com
5   "Child Advocate Diane Sowden Among Order of Canada Honourees" CBC Radio, The Current, December 30, 2021.
6   Tiana Sharifi and Sexual Exploitation Education (SEE). sexualexploitationeducation.com
7   Criminal Intelligence Service Canada (CISC) Organized Crime and Domestic Trafficking in Persons in Canada Strategic Intelligence Brief, August 2008.
8   Stop Trafficking Project (USA) with President and Founder Russ Tuttle. stoptraffickingproject.com
9   Canadian Women's Foundation, 2014 Report. This is an exceptional report and is worth reading closely. It gives an accurate landscape on the issue in Canada. Native Women's Associations, 2016 Report. Another excellent report detailing specifics, research and testimonies.
10 "Prostitution and Trafficking in Nine Countries: An Update on Violence and Post Traumatic Stress Disorder" by Melissa Farley. prostitutionresearch.com
11 "Brief to the Standing Committee on Justice and Human Rights and Review of The Protection of Communities and Exploited Persons Act" by Dr. Ingeborg Kraus, February 2022.
    One Child, a multiple award-winning organization dedicated to empowering a movement of children and youth to lead the fight against exploitation of children. The theme is, "One child exploited is one child too many." onechild.ca

CHAPTER 8

A Public Health Crisis

"In prostitution I acquiesced
to my trauma. I complied to the
grooming. I abdicated autonomy
in my body because my autonomy
was already taken."

SURVIVOR AARON CROWLEY
Author of "Bought with a Price"

"Take care of your body. It's the only
place you have to live."

JIM ROHN

Human trafficking victims are seen in the emergency room. Doctors in the ER are in a unique position to interact with trafficked persons. Doctors need to be able to assess trafficking indicators, collaborate with multidisciplinary service providers, ensure there is access to local provincial and federal resources to manage care and collaborate with law enforcement, educators and other health providers. Documentation is very important because there is an alarming lack of data and reporting in Canada.

When I started making presentations to raise awareness about human sex trafficking, sexual exploitation and child sex trafficking in B.C., I met a doctor who explained her experience in the emergency room. She could recognize victims but nine out of ten times the women would not report the sexual assault. Women and girls would tell the doctor, "No one believes me because I am on the street, and I use drugs." These victims feel it is their fault, their problem. They have deep shame and are desperately afraid to report. They typically cannot recall events for two to three days after the assault experience, which is called post-traumatic amnesia. Therefore the doctor suggests to wait for seventy-two hours before asking any questions. There is a high risk of sexual assault when a woman is homeless. With sleepless nights, homeless women are very vulnerable and will make frequent hospital visits to get to safety.

In the emergency room, the doctor and her team screen children for physical and sexual abuse. The signs of sexual abuse are night terrors, trouble sleeping, decreased appetite, trouble swallowing, mood swings (rage, fear, anger, withdrawal), fear of places and people, chronic abdominal pain, immature behaviour for their age, sexualized behaviour, suddenly having money, cutting and burns on the body. Her observation is that 80% to 90% of women in the sex trade have a history of sexual abuse, often as children, and 60% of sexual assault victims come from the foster system. Drug addiction is common. These individuals live with an overwhelming sense of worthlessness.

The journey to recovery is complex and takes time. Mentoring and support is needed. Learning to build healthy relationships is vital. Survivors need to learn basic life skills. A focus on education is beneficial.

The doctor's observation is that the sex industry is growing and the public needs to know the indicators (Chapter 10). The common myths of prostituted trafficked individuals are:

- They choose this.
- They enjoy this.
- There is no human trafficking in Canada, let alone in our neighbourhoods.
- This would never happen in my family.

I have made presentations in hospitals, meeting doctors, nurses and frontline health providers. In the process, I learned about the forensic nursing program offered through the Fraser Health Authority. FHA just celebrated thirty years of their Forensic Nursing Service, [1] which was the first of its kind in B.C. and second in Canada. Their goal is to educate nurses on how to gather legal forensic evidence while providing supportive, confidential nursing care to victims of sexual violence. Sexual Assault Nurse Examiners (SANE) provide trauma-informed victim-centred medical and forensic care to individuals who have experienced intentional person-to-person violence. Their vision is to have a cohesive network of health care providers across Canada working to advocate awareness of human trafficking and its impact on the heath of a person and the health care system.

Medical practitioners have not had specific training in human sex trafficking, yet it is rapidly becoming a public health crisis. During the two years of COVID-19, human sex trafficking increased significantly, and has become a behind-the-scenes shadow pandemic. Youth ended up with significantly more screen time, becoming highly vulnerable for predation online.

The sexual exploitation of youth and children is becoming widespread in society but more than often, the adults around them do not recognize it. There is a growing and significant increase of victims, and some are very young.

There is intersectionality with sex trafficking and domestic violence. For example, Alexandra Stevenson, the Laughing Survivor (Chapter 23), did not understand she was being trafficked, although her relationship with her boyfriend was very violent and abusive. She thought she was experiencing domestic violence and did not understand she was being trafficked.

Canada as a nation is beginning to recognize the rapidly growing issue of child sexual exploitation. There is the Canadian Centre to Protect Children (C3P, Manitoba), the National Human Trafficking Education Centre (NHTEC; Joy Smith Foundation in Manitoba) and the Canadian Centre to End Human Trafficking (CCTEHT, Ottawa) which operates the National Human Trafficking Hotline number at 1-833-900-1010. It is a 24/7 service, in multiple languages with trained social workers answering the calls. This resource is available for all residents in Canada. There is help for anyone in Canada.

There has been comparatively little attention given to trafficked persons in the healthcare system. With education and awareness, this can change. Human trafficking is under reported yet at some point most trafficked victims will access medical care. There is clearly an important opportunity here to reach and help victims. Victims that access the ER will report at least one physical health problem, have substance abuse problems which is a coping mechanism to survive the abuse, have STIs and report psychological issues. Some report trying to commit suicide.

Trafficked individuals typically do not have primary healthcare, pre-existing health conditions are neglected, they have ongoing exposure to communicable diseases, live with occupational and environmental hazards, experience economic abuse, have legal insecurity and are completely marginalized. These are some of the most neglected and desperate individuals in our society. Forensic Nursing intersects with the justice system and can provide evidence to press charges against sexual perpetrators, yet Canada is slow on prosecutions.

Sex traffickers are highly organized and sophisticated in their luring of victims. Traffickers first offer to provide basic survival needs and then they provide a distorted version of providing for higher needs to manipulate victims. Health providers need to begin with the basics, supplying food, water, shelter and clothing. They also need to screen for violence. To screen specifically for human trafficking, more intimate questions may need to be asked and that is a job for a trained social worker. The challenge is that social workers may lack training on human trafficking.

The trauma bonds (Stockholm Syndrome) are very deep. The victims literally fall in love with their perpetrators, so it becomes very difficult, if not impossible for them to leave their situations. In the case of each survivor that I got to know—Karen, Sarah, and Alexandra—they were only freed from their trafficker when those men died.

Surprisingly, women traffickers are very dangerous and more enticing than male traffickers. Victims will trust these female traffickers more readily. The recent case of Ghislaine Maxwell, [2] charged for grooming and sex trafficking girls for pedophile financier Jeffrey Epstein, is a troubling example. Peer on peer recruiting is becoming too common in high schools. Even in middle schools, females are found recruiting their girlfriends. It is very difficult for victims to disclose about their abuse. It is too painful for them. Health providers have a unique opportunity to help if they can recognize psychological and physical trafficking indicators.

For example, traffickers will use a form of branding (tattoos) to show their ownership of victims. Common tattoos are crowns, diamonds or the initials of the trafficker. Names of the trafficker are sometimes tattooed in backwards, so the girls see the name in the mirror. For many girls, their trafficker is their boyfriend and they do not realize they are being trafficked. He might be a lousy boyfriend, but at least he is a boyfriend. Sometimes the girls use the terms *my protector*, *my man* or *my king*.

There are push and pull factors[3] into the sex industry that health practitioners need to be aware of, so they can identify victims. Vulnerabilities make up the main push factors. Poverty, lack of human rights, unemployment, lack of social or economic opportunity, lack of education, violence from family dysfunction, adverse childhood experiences, gender-based inequality, sexual orientation, racism, corruption, war and conflict, political and civil unrest when violence results, migration, rural and remote living all contribute to pushing women into the industry.

As violence at home escalates, so does the urge to escape and run. If there is violence in childhood, that violence often becomes normalized to the individual. Abused mothers have huge impacts on their own children. Generational trauma develops and a devastating cycle of abuse continues. Aboriginal girls are over-represented in the sex industry, and they experience higher levels of violence.

The pull factors are the yearning for love and acceptance, the promise of a better life, the internet luring, financial rewards, employment, access to material benefit and migration.

Globally, there is a growing demand for sexual services. This contributes to a modern-day slave trade now developing in most countries. Recognizing the human trafficking indicators (Chapter 10) is a first step. Front-line identification of a person who is potentially trafficked is crucial.

Observing the presentation of the patient is important. Patient assessment involves looking at what the patient is wearing and getting the backstory of why the patient is there. Evaluate who is accompanying the patient. Has the patient come before? Is the accompaniment violent? Controlling? Do they have employer insurance? Where do they live? Do they have next of kin? Next of kin should be a family member, not a boyfriend. Are they working excessive hours? The key to a successful interaction is a trauma informed and patient centred approach in a safe environment. It is important to understand the mindset of the trafficked person.

Scientists are studying the neurobiology of trauma experiences, and learning that the brain becomes hypersensitive, unable to plan or think things thoroughly and memories become fragmented. It takes seventy-two hours for stress hormones to be released, which is two normal sleep cycles to bring back memory. When a trafficked person experiences a threat, survival reflexes are activated and show fight, flight, collapsed immobility (go floppy and almost pass out), habitual self-protection behaviours and lack of speech develop.[4]

In a global context, Dr. Ingeborg Kraus from Germany (Chapter 27) is a clinical psychologist, leading scientist and expert in the world in psychotraumatology. As a trauma expert, speaking and documenting her work with women victims of sexual violence, she has organized scientists towards a world without prostitution. Dr. Kraus is breaking the silence around the issue of prostitution, specifically in Germany, where she seeks to abolish prostitution. She closely analyzes trauma and the severity of PTSD. She states that sexual violence is the most serious form of trauma in her brief submitted to the Federal Justice Committee in February 2022. Sexual harm is a huge worldwide problem and a huge cost to the health care system. Her observation is that we live in a world of rape.

Her question in Germany where prostitution is legalized, "Is prostitution violence or a service?" In Germany, 5% of prostituted persons are German; 95% come from elsewhere. Dr. Kraus is concerned about the lies perpetuated about prostitution, that it is a job like any other. To allow strangers to penetrate the body, women must completely shut down or switch themselves off. This is complete dissociation from self. Because sexual and physical violence is very high in prostitution, PTSD and accompanying dissociations are very common. Trauma affects every part of the being. The good news, according to Dr. Kraus is that it is possible to recover. Psycho-education to treat trauma is very important and this is the work and focus of Dr. Kraus both in Germany and internationally.

Disassociation is a trance-like state when the identity is affected and the woman plays a role. At some point this ability to disassociate fails and becomes a lasting state and the woman switches off. The goal of psycho trauma therapy is for feelings and senses to return and for a realization of personal autonomy, agency and identity to return.

Women and girls can learn very young to switch off especially with childhood trauma, sexual abuse or incest. Trauma memory is like a black box that we do not have access to; it has no sense of space or time and no language but can be brought on by numerous triggers. When triggered it causes PTSD or flashbacks. This is literally a time bomb in the head, and there is no warning or preparation for the bomb exploding. Trauma can be a deep and unpredictable fear reaction.

When sexual violence is ongoing, there is a deeper level of complex trauma called complex PTSD. Complex PTSD trauma symptoms include flashbacks, nightmares, being easily frightened, development of avoiding behaviours, hyper vigilance, inability to trust anyone and the inability to feel love or happiness. There are predominately negative thoughts and there is often a developing preoccupation with suicide. There is hyper arousal, a tendency to be very nervous, ongoing sleep disorders and accompanying high-risk behaviour. The self can become 'marinated' in abandonment and a deep sense of shame may develop.

There is an inability to regulate emotions so depression, disorders of personality, eating disorders, cutting and self-destructive acts can occur. Addictions are common, resulting from self-medicating the pain. Victims blame themselves and lose the ability to see what a healthy relationship looks like. Bonding to the perpetrator occurs. The dynamic of trauma says, "You have no choice." The important door to open for these individuals is, "You have a choice." The essentials of Trauma Informed Care (TIC) are: [5]

- Connect: to focus on relationships.
- Protect: to promote safety and trustworthiness.
- Respect: to engage in choice and collaboration.
- Redirect: to encourage skill building and competence.

Dr. Kraus's conclusion: There is no "good" prostitution because all prostitution is violence. This is the conclusion and summary of the Canadian PCEPA Law as well, clearly stated in the preamble (Appendix A).

Researching this topic for almost a decade, I have heard an increasing number of experiences of incest from survivors. Father-daughter abuse is thought of as most common, but sibling abuse is surprisingly high and can last for years. Marginalized communities are most affected by incest. The incest dynamic involves:

- Reliance on the offender.
- Generational abuse.
- Isolation and the family rally around the perpetrator.
- There is a confusing overlap of abuse and love.
- The questions become: What is true love?
- Relationships continue beyond the abuse. How are those handled within families?
- The child is blamed.

- There is denial from other family members.
- The damage is downplayed.
- "Forgive and forget" is the mantra.
- There are threats and coercion to keep the secret.

More information, statistics and solutions can be found online at incestaware.org.

Endnotes

1 Forensic Nursing Service at Fraser Health Authority in British Columbia providing trauma-informed medical and forensic care to individuals who have experienced recent sexual assault and or intentional relationship violence. They provide an online module at fraserhealth.ca called Human Trafficking: Help Don't Hinder. They are part of the Human Trafficking Health Alliance of Canada and Health Education Advocacy Linkage (HEAL Trafficking). healtrafficking.org
Dr. Nadine Burke Harris, "How Childhood Trauma Affects Health Across a Lifetime" ted.com
2 "Ghislaine Maxwell Sentenced to 20 Years for Helping Jeffrey Epstein Sexually Abuse Teenage Girls" CBC News, June 28, 2022.
3 Push and Pull Factors directly influence and perpetuate human sex trafficking structures: United Nations Office on Drugs and Crime, published 2019. sextraffickingrogers.weebly.com
VAWnet.org (Violence Against Women), a project of the National Resource Center on Domestic Violence, published September 1, 2014.
4 Trauma Bonds from the Province of B.C. www2.gov.bc.ca
"The Bond That Harms: The Impact of Trauma Bonding on Human Trafficking Victims" by Yvette Young. forbes.com
"Trauma Bonding in Human Trafficking" from Office to Monitor and Combat Trafficking in Persons, June 2020, Washington, DC. www.state.gov/wp-content/uploads/2020/10/TIP_Factsheet-Trauma-Bonding-in-Human-Trafficking-508.pdf
5 Humner V., Crosland K., Dollard, N. 2009

CHAPTER 9

Frontline Service Providers

"You treat a disease, you win, you lose.
You treat a person, I guarantee you,
you'll win, no matter what the outcome."

PATCH ADAMS

Frontline service providers ask me to give educational seminars because they recognize there is a public health problem in their communities that is not being addressed. Sexual exploitation is a rapidly growing scourge. Youth, children and the vulnerable are being aggressively targeted. Communities cannot be healthy, thriving or safe where there is sexual exploitation taking place.

The first question I am asked is, "What can we do to stop sexual exploitation in our communities?" It is critical to raise awareness about the issue, internally and externally with partners, clients, staff and stakeholders.

- Learn the indicators of human trafficking.
- Know the numbers to call for help and advice.
- Make sure the workplace is trauma-informed (Chapter 8).
- Have a code of conduct for all staff.

- The most important question to ask anyone who you think is in difficulty is not, "What is wrong with you?" but instead, "What happened to you?"

There are several strategies to stop exploitation. Providing jobs, internships and skills training for youth, to keep them out of the sex industry is critical. Providing these opportunities for survivors, helps them get their lives back on track. It is vital to role model to men and boys the importance of not exploiting women and girls, emphasizing the importance of respect, integrity and healthy relationships while upholding the principles of gender equality and human rights in all interactions. Consider having a code of conduct in your work environment for your employees, staff and partners. Take action in the community, be a part of awareness campaigns, collaborate with NGOs and collaborate with those on the frontline in other communities, provincially and nationally.

Work with law enforcement. Keep them in the loop of any suspicious activity. Encourage them to get additional training; for example, I presented at the first RCMP cross-country webinar series on human trafficking that was available for every officer and police agency in the country. That is something local officers can request and sign up for.

Collaborate with businesses that can hire, mentor and train youth to work. Learning and taking responsibility is a significant step into the adult world and will help youth develop into resilient, contributing, healthy citizens in a community. Business experience and training is invaluable for learning life skills. The alternative may be gang life or criminal activity, and communities must stop this growing trend.

The key to stopping sexual exploitation is a cultural and societal shift in how men and boys view women and girls, so they understand healthy relationships with a focus on respect and integrity. One female survivor told me, "The onus cannot be on the girls to protect themselves; boys need to be taught the steps, using their privilege and power for good." She suggested creating a space for men and boys with positive role modeling. The Moosehide Campaign[1] is a good example. It is an Indigenous initiative for men and boys to learn to protect the women and girls in their lives. The Boys Club Network[2] is an after school program—with pizza provided!—in the Lower Mainland that was started by Walter Mustapich, a former inner city high school teacher and administrator. At risk boys are mentored by successful businessmen and athletes and are taught to respect the women and girls in their lives. Hopefully other groups and agencies will develop this focus on promoting healthy masculinity so that boys have an alternative to the toxic masculine role models promoted in our culture. The best model for addressing human sex trafficking, sexual exploitation and child sex trafficking is strong, compassionate, well-supported law enforcement and an ongoing public awareness campaign.

"Every young person is one caring and consistent adult away from success." A young survivor and now teen expert and youth speaker Josh Shipp made this statement. Josh says, "Every child who winds up doing well has had at least one stable and committed relationship with a supportive adult."[3]

It is possible to turn back the dial and help marginalized vulnerable youth as Kelly Tallon Franklin states in her survivor advocacy work with her organization Courage for Freedom.[4] Kelly effectively uses equine therapy to reach and help young survivors get their lives back on track.

The growing problem in Canadian cities right now is the significant spike in crime. Consider Vancouver and Surrey as examples.[5] These downtown cores have an increasing amount of homelessness, drug use, prostitution, out of control gang growth and tent cities. It has become impossible for many businesses to operate. Public safety is the job of provincial and municipal officials because they mandate policies and determine the priorities for the funding of local law enforcement.

Principle: safe communities are good for everyone.

Parents are the main influencers in a child's life and therefore the most important allies for frontline service providers. Working with parents is strategic because they know their children the best. Sadly, some parents are also the traffickers and sexual exploiters. This is an issue that also must be addressed.

How can parents protect their children? The key for parents is to create a secure attachment because it is important to have connection, trust, with reasonable attainable expectations. This will build resiliency in youth. Parents must be engaged, set limits, not assume everything is okay, have open dialogue and know where to turn for help.

Prevention is the best strategy. Keeping children and youth out of the sex industry is the first step. Children of the Street (PLEA) has excellent programs reaching grades three to twelve students in B.C. Sex Exploitation Education or SEE by Tiana Sharifi offers training. Joy Smith has launched the National Human Trafficking Education Centre out of Manitoba.

Exit services are generally lacking and 24/7 wraparound services are needed to keep people out of the sex industry, otherwise they slip back into it. A good example in Vancouver is Deborah's Gate with the Salvation Army and Covenant House for underage trafficked homeless youth. Prostituted persons will stay in the industry when they see no way out. Drug detox is the first step. Trauma bonds/Stockholm Syndrome are deep (Chapter 8), so this is part of the complex PTSD that needs to be addressed.

Human sex trafficking and sexual exploitation is everyone's problem yet public awareness in British Columbia is generally lacking. Some provinces in Canada such as Alberta, Manitoba, Ontario and Nova

Scotia are more proactive in providing public awareness and law enforcement training.

There are concerning trends developing. Child-on-child sexual assault is on the rise. Virtual reality platforms (Metaverse) can show sexual assault of adults and children, which has the same impact on the brain as physical assault. Sexting, cyberbullying, cyber-sex terrorism are becoming more common. The recently concluded Amanda Todd case in B.C. is an illustrative and frightening example.[6] Amanda was the fifteen-year-old who killed herself as a result of a cyberbullying campaign against her by a Dutch man who harassed and extorted her. Before her death she posted a video using a series of flashcards to tell her experience of being blackmailed by using her webcam. The video went viral after her death with 15 million views as of January 2023.

Endnotes

1   "Standing Up Against Violence Towards Women and Children" from Moose Hide Campaign Development Society. moosehidecampaign.ca
    Joint statement on Moose Hide Campaign Day, BC Premier, May 12, 2022. news.gov.bc.ca
2   "Growing At-Risk Boys Into Good Men" by Walter Mustapich, November 3, 2015. Boys Club Network: In a perfect world all boys would have hope, opportunity, positive mentorship, education. boysclubnetwork.com/tedx/
3   "Foster Care to Harvard University" by Josh Shipp, award-winning speaker and best-selling author. joshshipp.com
4   Kelly Tallon Franklin with Courage for Freedom in Ontario, a survivor-led, community-based registered incorporated charity with a mission to eradicate human trafficking and sexual exploitation of girls, boys and children. courageforfreedom.org
5   "Child sex trafficking is on the rise in Canada" podcast interview with Harpreet Singh and Cathy Peters, May 10, 2022. vancouver.redfm.ca/child-sex-trafficking-is-on-the-rise-in-canada/
6   Amanda Todd Legacy Society. Videos and documentaries are on this website explaining the case, in hopes of educating parents, youth and children about sextortion. amandatoddlegacy.org

CHAPTER 10

Indicators of Sex Trafficking

"The Blue Heart represents the sadness of those who are trafficked while reminding us of the cold-heartedness of those who buy and sell fellow human beings. The use of the blue UN colour also demonstrates the commitment of the United Nations to combating this crime against human dignity."

UNITED NATIONS OFFICE ON DRUGS AND CRIME,
THE BLUE HEART CAMPAIGN AGAINST HUMAN TRAFFICKING

Recognizing potential red flags and knowing the indicators of human trafficking is a key step in identifying victims and helping them find the assistance they need.[1] Trafficking victims are kept in bondage through a combination of fear, intimidation, abuse, and psychological controls including addiction. Trafficking victims live a life marked by abuse, betrayal of their basic human rights, and control under their trafficker.

Most trafficking victims will not readily volunteer information about their status because of the fear and abuse they have suffered at the hands of their trafficker. They may also be reluctant to come forward with information from despair, discouragement, and a sense that there are no viable options to escape their situation. Even if pressed, they may not identify themselves as someone held in bondage for fear of retribution to themselves or family members. However, there are indicators that point to a person held in a slavery condition.

The following indicators may not be enough to meet the legal standard for trafficking, but they indicate that someone else controls a victim and the situation should be further investigated. This list represents only a selection of possible indicators.

Possible work and living conditions of a trafficked individual:
- Is under eighteen-years-old and is providing commercial sex acts.
- Minor with older boyfriend/girlfriend.
- Fake ID, lies about age.
- Claims of being an adult although appearance suggests adolescent features.
- Presence of different aliases and ages.
- Has a pimp or manager that controls the money.
- Is unpaid, paid very little, or paid only through tips.
- The victim will have very little or no pocket money.
- Have few or no personal possessions.
- Does not hold his/her own identity or travel documents.
- Is not allowed to speak for themselves; a third party may insist on being present and/or translating.
- Claims they are just visiting and are unable to clarify where he/she is staying or at what address.
- Lack of knowledge of whereabouts and/or do not know what city he/she is in.
- Residency is a hotel or motel.
- Loss of sense of time.

- Has numerous inconsistencies in his/her story.
- Speaks as though citing from a script.
- Works excessively long and/or unusual hours.
- Is not allowed breaks or suffers under unusual restrictions at work.
- Was recruited through false promises concerning the nature and conditions of his/her work.
- Owes a large debt and is unable to pay it off.
- Is not free to leave or come and go as he/she wishes.
- High security measures exist in the work and/or living locations, for example opaque windows, boarded-up windows, bars on windows, barbed wire, security cameras.
- Victims live at the same premises as the brothel or "work site" or are driven between quarters and work by a guard. For labour trafficking, victims are often prohibited from leaving the work site, which may look like a guarded compound from the outside.
- Victims are kept under surveillance when taken to a doctor, hospital or clinic for treatment; trafficker may act as a translator.
- High foot traffic of men arriving and leaving the premises where there may be trafficked women.
- Women are not seen leaving the premises unless escorted.

Health characteristics of a trafficked person:
Trafficked individuals may be treated as disposable possessions without much attention given to their mental or physical health. Accordingly, some of the health problems that may be evident in a victim include:
- Displays symptoms of malnutrition, dehydration or poor personal hygiene and lacks basic healthcare.
- Exhibits sexual behaviour that is not developmentally appropriate.
- Contracts sexually transmitted diseases.

- Demonstrates signs of physical abuse, sexual abuse, confinement, or torture, bruising, broken bones, cigarette burns on body, scarring, scrapes, scratches, black eyes, or other signs of untreated medical problems.
- Develops critical illnesses including diabetes, cancer or heart disease.
- Experiences post-traumatic stress or psychological disorders.
- Suffers from verbal or psychological abuse designed to intimidate, degrade and frighten the individual.
- Is fearful, anxious, depressed, submissive, tense, nervous or paranoid.
- Experiences memory loss.
- Behaviour becomes erratic, with severe mood swings.
- Suffers drug and alcohol addiction.
- Exhibits tattooing or branding symbols such as names on the neck, wrists or lower back.
- Exhibits unusually fearful or anxious behaviour after speaking about law enforcement.
- Avoids eye contact.

Fraser Health Authority's Forensic Nursing Service has designed a human trafficking screening protocol with the following sample questions:
- What type of work do you do?
- Can you leave your job or situation if you want?
- Can you come and go as you please?
- Have you been threatened if you try to leave?
- Have you been physically harmed in any way?
- What are your working or living conditions like?
- Where do you sleep and eat; at home or at a work site?
- Do you sleep in a bed, cot, or on the floor?
- Have you been deprived of food, water, sleep, or medical care?

- Do you have to get permission to eat, sleep, or go to the bathroom?
- Are there locks on your doors and windows so you cannot get out?
- Has anyone threatened your family?
- Has your identification for documentation been taken from you?
- Is anyone forcing you to do anything that you do not want to do?

Some additional questions to ask to evaluate a victim's safety:
- Are you feeling safe right now?
- Is it safe for me to talk to you?
- Do you have any concerns for your safety?
- Will something bad happen to you or a family member if you leave?
- In the case of a foreign national: Why are you here?
- Is there anything I can do for you?

Anyone can report suspected trafficking cases. In the USA, if the victim is under eighteen years old, professionals who work in law enforcement, healthcare, social care, mental health, and education are mandated to report such cases.

Through a grassroots community-wide effort and public awareness campaign, more professionals on the front line can readily identify the trafficked victim and have him or her treated accordingly.

Learn more at humantraffickinghotline.org. Polaris Project operates this hotline and on this extensive website lists human trafficking indicators.

Frontline service providers and youth workers can ask the following questions:
- How are you?
- How did you meet this person?
- How do you know them?

- Why don't you want to go home?
- What makes this place and these people feel safe for you?
- Are there any family or supports that we can connect with? If so, who?
- What resources can I offer?

The key is to get the youth connected to something positive. Trafficking will occur anywhere that youth congregate, especially online. Offline, this can be at public transit, shopping malls, Airbnbs, hotels, at schools, community centres, foster and group homes, shelters and safe houses, youth drop-in centres, youth detox and treatment centres.

Student indicators:
- Skipping school and classes.
- Unexplained absences, especially on Thursdays and Fridays.
- A sudden withdrawal from friends or classmates.
- Urgency to respond to phone.
- Exhausted.
- Wearing new clothes, nails done, lashes, expensive purse.
- Unexpected material possessions given to them by a "friend."
- Sudden change in attire.
- Multiple cellphones.
- Extreme change in online behaviour; suddenly online all the time or not interested in being online.
- Has an older boyfriend. Focuses on boyfriend and the boyfriend's behaviour.
- Isolating.
- Unhealthy changes.
- A gut feeling from parents, service providers, teachers that something is wrong.

- Drops out of school.
- Wears expensive clothing, jewellery they cannot afford.
- Involved in a gang or criminal activity such as drugs or theft.
- Fears for their safety.
- Secretive. Reluctant to share where they have been and with whom.
- States boyfriend or girlfriend tells them who they can or cannot spend time with, what they can wear, controls their phone.
- Talk of "clubbing" or dancing.
- Talk of travel or going somewhere outside of the city.

Endnotes

1   United Nations Office on Drugs and Crime: Human Trafficking Indicators. www.unodc.org

"Indicators of Human Trafficking" Department of Homeland Security, US Government Blue Campaign. A national public awareness campaign designed to educate the public, law enforcement and industry partners to recognize the indicators of human trafficking and how to respond. dhs.gov

"Signs of Human Trafficking" Canadian Centre to End Human Trafficking. canadiancentretoendhumantrafficking.ca

"What Are The Signs That Someone May Be Trafficked? #KnowTheSigns" Joy Smith Foundation. joysmithfoundation.com

CHAPTER 11

Survivors

"The officers remembered my birthday, so I let them help me. No one had ever remembered my birthday."

A SURVIVOR

"Without men's demand for prostitute women, there would be no such women"

SVEN-AXEL MANSSON, SWEDEN 2003

"It is easy to get in and hard to get out."

A SURVIVOR

In 2014, the Protection of Communities and Exploited Persons Act (PCEPA) became federal law in Canada.[1] Before the law was enacted, it had to be approved by both the Federal Justice Committee and the Senate of Canada. After listening to hours of the hearings, what stood out to me were the testimonies of survivors, the women who had exited prostitution. Here are some of the stories and testimonies that convinced me that this law needs to be strengthened, upheld, and enforced in Canada.[2]

Natashe Falle is the co-founder and managing director of Sextrade 101, a survivor-led political activism coalition.[3] She has trained police and frontline agency workers on the issues of sex trafficking, prostitution, and organized crime.

Her father was a police officer and her mother ran a bridal shop. When her parents divorced, her new single parent home became unsafe and she ran away. She became involved in the sex industry in Calgary at age fifteen. She was involved in the sex trade for ten years, suffering extreme trauma, violence and torture. Fourteen and fifteen-year-old girls introduced her to The Game and then she introduced her five underage friends to prostitution. Prostitution was glamorized initially. She did not have a pimp or take drugs at first, but all her friends eventually gained pimps and became addicted to drugs. While she was underage, it was very easy for her to get work.

Natasha experienced work with hundreds of other underage girls. She managed to get out of prostitution in desperation for a better life. She states that prostitution is not a commercial exchange or transaction, rather, it is sustained trauma and brutalization. Once in, it is not a choice, it is slavery. Her definition of a real choice is that you must have realistic options.

Casandra Diamond[4] is a leading advocate in addressing human trafficking in Canada. Growing up she felt lonely, powerless and unloved. When Casandra was seventeen years of age, a friend invited her to work in a strip club as an easy way to make money. That strip club became the gateway to the dark industry of prostitution where she saw twelve to fourteen men a night. She was punched, slapped and beaten, all in the name of a job. Her story is not an uncommon one in Canada.

In her 2020 TEDx Toronto talk, with over three million views titled, "I was sex trafficked for years. Brothels are hidden in plain sight," she shares her story about her experience in prostitution. In her ten years as a prostituted woman, she always worked for organized crime and criminals. There was no personal choice; there was no self-dignity, no hope, and no safe place to turn. No one she worked with enjoyed it. She states that municipal licensing of massage parlours normalizes prostitution and renders it invisible and underground. Indoor facilities where she was exploited are run by organized crime and the profit is huge. During that time, she worked with only one aboriginal girl as they do not make it indoors. A single trafficker will control a stable of young victims; mostly white and Asian girls. The aboriginal girls tend to work on the streets. It is highly discriminatory. Screening is impossible. For Casandra, aging out was her exit strategy.

In 2014, Casandra founded BridgeNorth Women's Mentorship and Advocacy Services in Ontario, dedicated to ending sex trafficking in Canada. The organization provides holistic care to exploited and trafficked persons through prevention strategies, exit strategies and safety planning. Casandra currently advises the province of Ontario and municipalities on anti-human trafficking strategies.

From her experience, indoor prostitution—massage parlours, strip clubs and brothels versus girls who work on the street—has less choice, because there is no opportunity for a girl to say *No*. There is more pimp control, yet it is considered more socially acceptable. It is romanticized because it is out of sight.

From her experience, organized crime and gangs have trafficking operations in unregistered massage parlours. Her anti-trafficking efforts focus on stopping the licensing of them; emphasizing the importance of safe communities. From her extensive years involved in prostitution, she explains that prostitution is paid rape. Yet in Canada there are rules, regulations and laws stating it is against the law to rape.

Casandra unequivocally states that prostitution is dehumanizing, coercive and that there is no safe place in prostitution. It is sex slavery run by organized crime, which will increase into more organized crime worldwide. Prostitution is not work. She was regularly exposed to STIs, HIV, and potential physical, emotional, and mental harm resulting in PTSD. Her experience is a typical example of the extreme violence and exploitation that is the norm for women in prostitution.

She observed the trend of younger and younger girls getting involved. Friending tactics are used to target girls, often by other girls. Gangs target group homes. The girls who are prostituted get no money; the pimps, traffickers and organized groups keep the money.

Casandra is concerned that the new epidemic impacting prostitution is porn addiction where rough sex and violence are glorified, and women are portrayed as enjoying it.

Katarina McLeod,[5] the founder of Rising Angels, was in the sex trade for fifteen years. She had been sexually abused as a child. She entered at twenty-one years of age because she lacked options and a sense of self-worth. She experienced sexual and physical abuse, drug addiction, forcible confinement, domestic prostitution, and trafficking. Once she entered The Game it was very difficult to leave. The Game or The Life are terms that describe the subculture of prostitution, complete with rules, a hierarchy of authority and language. The term gives the illusion that it can be a fun and easy way to make money, when the reality is much harsher. Katarina states that ensuring safety in prostitution is impossible and her concern is that men do not understand the negative effect and harm on women.

Linda and Ed Smith[6] from Regina, Saskatchewan lost their daughter Sherry Lynn Smith in 1990 at eighteen years old to sex trafficking.

Sherry grew up in a happy home and was known for her musical talent and leadership qualities. She met her seventeen-year-old boyfriend who had a $400 per day drug habit. She ran away with him, saying she loved him. Days later she ended up in Edmonton, servicing men, romanced by her boyfriend, and then beaten. Sherry would do anything to keep her boyfriend. She was moved from Calgary, to Winnipeg, then Regina, and finally Victoria. She developed an STI and became malnourished but she would not leave her boyfriend/pimp. The police apprehended her twice and sent her home, but she kept returning to her boyfriend. The parents could do nothing because her pimp psychologically controlled Sherry. By this point she had no choices. Hundreds of men abused her. No man was ever charged, and her pimp, loverboy boyfriend was never charged because Sherry would not testify against any of them. The Smiths stated this is not an uncommon experience for many families. Sherry was found pregnant and beaten to death in Victoria. No one was ever charged with the murder.

Linda Smith developed a presentation for grades six to eight, making hundreds of presentations. The Smith's wish is for more education, so youth would not get pulled into The Game. Ed Smith spoke at "John Schools" to educate the apprehended buyers of sex of the harm and damage they do to families and to the women they hire. The purpose of a John School is to educate and deter men who have been the customers of prostitutes. Ed asked johns why they started to buy sex. Every man he spoke with said they began by viewing pornography—it was the fuel. At the end of their presentations to the Federal Justice Committee, Ed Smith was asked, "Can we eradicate prostitution?" Ed answered, "We must do everything we can to set the captives free." At this point Ed Smith broke down and wept.

Glendene Grant is founder of MATH,[7] Mothers Against Trafficking Humans and mother of Jessie Foster who is considered Canada's poster child for the crime of human trafficking. Jessie became an international endangered missing woman and was one of the most publicized human trafficking victims in Canada.

Originally from Kamloops, Jessie was the second daughter of four in a loving family. She was an honours student; into sports, music and dance. She was a successful young woman who had a lot of friends. She was never in any kind of trouble.

At seventeen years of age, Jessie met a man in Calgary who became her friend. In retrospect it became clear that this man was grooming Jessie. He took her on trips to Florida and then to New York, ending up in Las Vegas. He suggested to her that she prostitute herself because funds had run out and there was no money for expenses to get home. Jessie phoned home at this point. She kept in touch with her mother, but her story kept changing. Ultimately, Jessie chose to stay in Las Vegas and moved in with the man she had fallen in love with. Then she disappeared and was never found.

The trauma and suffering endured by Glendene and her family has been ongoing. Glendene speaks publicly to raise awareness. Raising awareness about human trafficking has become a personal crusade for her and is her coping mechanism. When Jessie went missing, human trafficking was not a well-known crime. The public did not believe human trafficking occurred in Canada. Glendene speaks out so that Canadians can understand that it does happen in Canada.

Bridget Perrier[8] is a co-founder of Sextrade 101 along with Natasha Falle. She had experienced child sexual abuse before a family adopted her. She was lured into prostitution at twelve, and for the next ten years was prostituted. She states that her body was invaded for ten years. She was paraded with other girls like cattle, and in the end was discarded like a piece of tissue. She now lives with psychological trauma, is angry and feels cheated. She lives with haunting john memories. She cannot have children naturally because of chronic pelvic pain but is now stepmother to Angel, whose biological mother was Brenda Wolfe, one of Robert Pickton's murder victims.

She serviced shipmen when she was thirteen. At fourteen she was raped and tortured for forty-three hours straight. She fought for her life. Her first pimp was a woman. Her second pimp was her bodyguard, a man who specialized in selling little girls, and the girls that are the most in demand by the johns. She stated, "Johns are very savvy, they know what they want and they get it." Bridget added, "Having a legal bawdy house is not going to make it any safer. You are still going to attract serial killers, rapists and perverts."[9] Her question to the Federal Justice Committee, "If prostitution is such a healthy activity, why don't johns tell their wives, families and children what they are doing?" She ended her presentation with, "Women are sacred and loved and we are equal." At this point the room burst into clapping.

Bridget Perrier referred to the article by renowned medical researcher Dr. Vincent J. Felitti who made the connection between childhood experiences and physical and mental health as adults.[10] Dr. Felitti addresses how childhood trauma is associated with chronic diseases during adulthood and how child trafficking will eventually worsen the economic burden on civil governance. As an example, Bridget pointed out that she would watch young native girls brought to parties where they were sexually pulverized. The native girls were blamed that it was their fault and never reported the rapes. She pointed out that the harm caused by these rapes would be part of the psyche of the girls, for their whole lives.

Marina Giacomin is a survivor who worked with Servants Anonymous (SAS). At sixteen she frequented the Downtown Eastside in Vancouver. Prostitution for Marina became the ultimate sexual abuse. After she became free from prostitution, she became a social worker with

Servants Anonymous Society in Calgary. SAS offers a SAFE program for an immediate exit from prostitution for girls and women. The SAFE program is professionally staffed 24/7, provides access to medical care, detoxification, and addiction services if required. Trauma recovery work begins there. It is a thirty to forty-five day stabilization program. Outcome statistics show that women remaining a minimum of four weeks in SAFE experience have a 90% success rate in exiting to safe and stable environments. SAS offers one of the most comprehensive exit programs in Canada. It is now called Reset Calgary.[11]

Service data on over 700 girls and women at SAS shows that 100% of prostituted girls experienced violence, 40% identify as aboriginal, and 90% were introduced to prostitution by fourteen years of age. These girls are voiceless and have no way to speak up. Exiting is virtually impossible, as one woman in the program explains, "The only way out of being pimped is either death or being sick with HIV, because if you are HIV positive, the bikers, gangs and violent johns will kill you themselves."

Marina stated to the Federal Justice Committee, "It is not a right to have sex. It is a right to not be exploited." Her concern for Canada is that if full decriminalization of prostitution were to occur, Canada would become a sex tourism destination for the USA because of the shared border.

Larissa Crack[12] was co-founder of the Northern Women's Connection and a survivor of sex trafficking. She was prostituted at fourteen by a thirty-year-old lover. She exited prostitution at seventeen years of age, and because she was still underage, she was able to access help and supports. If she had been nineteen, those supports would not have been available. At seventeen, she had poor mental health, was impoverished, lived with trauma and was drug addicted. Most indoor establishments from her experience involved organized crime. And the problem with indoor agencies is that no one knows you are there.

Larissa had been held at gunpoint, watched her friend get murdered, was tied down for days at a time, injected with numbing drugs while men paid to rape her. She had been beaten and thrown out of the vehicles of men who did not want to pay for the service they had received and suffered multiple injuries from the pimps if they did not receive their set rate of revenue. Violence has been and always will be associated with prostitution. But the deepest pain for Larissa is hearing others say that prostitution is a choice, is work and a job like any other.

Trisha Baptie,[13] founder of EVE, formerly Exploited Voices Now Educating, is an exited survivor from Vancouver who presented to the Federal and Senate Committees in 2014 as well as to the Federal Justice Committee in 2022. She experienced fifteen years in prostitution from ages thirteen to twenty-eight. The last ten years were in Vancouver's Downtown Eastside. She lost many friends to serial killer and john Willy Pickton. She worked indoors and outdoors and never had the choice of consent. Needing money does not equal consent. Men took advantage of her desperation. She stated, "No law beat and killed her friends, it was men. The location was never the issue, it was men." Her message is, "Women are not for sale and we value our women. This is the only job where you need exiting services and rehabilitation." This is because of the severe trauma that prostitution causes. The key is to change male behaviour; the demand that fuels the sex industry.

She felt the threat of violence was always there and possible. She is concerned that as a country we are setting the standard for how men will treat and view women. She asked the question, "Why should men have the right to have sex on their own terms at any time they want? This is rape culture." At her 2022 presentation to the Justice Committee she stated she would not use the term sex work because "it is not work but exploitation." The term also ignores the role of men, the perpetrators of sexual exploitation. She observes that young naive women are sought out specifically. Their age is getting younger; thirteen years old in the sex industry is common, particularly amongst her Indigenous friends. Yet, men are demanding younger girls. Her question, "How does men buying sex make a community safe?" She added that PCEPA is about ending a practice, not about hating sex workers. Social media, apps and social websites are a problem.

Timea Nagy[14] is a well-known international speaker on human trafficking. She is a tireless, articulate advocate for social change. When Timea came to Canada in 1998 she was forced into prostitution for three terrifying months. She was able to escape with the assistance of a police officer. Subsequently she founded the "Walk with Me" NGO to assist victims of human trafficking and educate law enforcement agencies. Timea played a key role in Canada's largest human trafficking investigation led by the RCMP, known as project OPAPA. Her memoir, *Out of the Shadows* released in 2019 became a national bestseller.[15] It is her firsthand account of the brutality and ugliness of human trafficking.

Timea presented at the Federal Justice Committee in 2014. She stated, "Don't call prostitution work. That is offensive to me." One to 10% are girls who choose prostitution; 90–98% of voices are not heard, and 60–90% were sexually molested as children. She also states, "Prostitution is oppression, not a profession." Every day in the sex industry she knew she could be hurt or killed. Her question, "Where do we want to go as a society?"

Timea presented at a law enforcement webinar series on human trafficking where I presented as well. During her presentation she went over the mindset of the victim. She shared her personal story and her family upbringing, which set the stage for her vulnerability. At twenty-one she answered an ad to come to Canada. Her home life was chaotic, witnessing the domestic violence of her parents before she suffered abuse from her brother. Her father left the home when she was nine years old. She was sexually assaulted at twelve, then again at thirteen and at sixteen years of age. She never told anyone. Her mind felt split, she felt dirty and like she was nothing. She was labelled as promiscuous, but she did not know what was wrong. She did not develop properly. She lived with constant anxiety.

Timea described Adverse Childhood Experiences (ACE) that include physical abuse, emotional abuse, sexual abuse, domestic violence, parental substance abuse, mental illness, suicide or death, crime or imprisoned family member. If a youth or child experiences five out of eight of these ACEs, they are especially vulnerable for abuse. This is a perfect storm for being sexually exploited.

From ages sixteen to twenty-one, Timea said she was on her own, raised herself, went to school, worked, and had a mean, abusive boyfriend. Her family got behind on paying the family bills and were at risk of losing their house. So, Timea accepted a job in Canada. She was so desperate, and it looked like a quick fix. Deep down she felt something was wrong, but she had no way to figure it out. She did not know how to make a healthy choice.

When she arrived in Canada, she was taken immediately to a strip club to perform. She became another personality with a different name. She was relocated and isolated, had little food and sleep, was threatened and was constantly emotionally and physically abused. In two to three weeks, her spirit was broken. Timea did not speak English and was trapped. In 1998, when this happened to her, there were no laws in Canada on human trafficking. Her childhood trauma had to be suppressed while she lived another level of trauma. She had no idea of the real world anymore. Timea had no way to speak up, and the trauma and pain were very deep.

The turning point for Timea was when a kind, calm police officer said to her, "How are you? Are you okay?" It was the first time she felt like she was treated as a human being. That was when she spoke up and got the help she desperately needed and wanted. She describes the six types of traffickers:

- Businessman.
- Female friend.
- Romeo (boyfriend).
- Gorilla (the most dangerous).
- A friend of a friend.
- Family.

She describes the stages of healing as:

- Denial: the girl or boy has no idea what is going on.
- Suspecting: the victim is still in denial, but police and frontline service providers can plant a seed and create doubt.
- Knowing: the victim still acts in denial but is quiet. She is not ready to leave The Game.
- Numb: she cannot feel anything. This is the time to speak with her and offer help.
- Ready to Talk: police and service providers need to go very slow at this point and go somewhere safe.
- Terrified: they know they are in trouble and that their trafficker will kill them if they find out that the girl is trying to leave. At this point officers and frontline service providers need to be kind and calm, provide emergency care and any immediate needs. This will be food, clothing, transportation, a place to sleep and to see a doctor. Trafficking victims are starving, physically and emotionally.

An effective educational resource I use in my youth presentations is Timea's YouTube music video, "Break the Silence" (Canadian version-January 30, 2013).

Andrea Heinz[16] presented at the Federal Justice Committee hearings in 2022 as an exited sex seller—she was never trafficked. Currently she is studying the impacts of violence against women and is a published scholar on the commercialized sex industry. She has spent a decade interacting with sex buyers attending the Edmonton sex trade offender program, training members and recruits in the Edmonton Police Service and speaking with those entering and exiting the sex industry. Prior to her work and education, she spent seven years in Edmonton's licensed and regulated sex industry from 2006 to 2013 (typically massage parlours until the introduction of PCEPA in 2014). At twenty-two, when she was drowning in debt and had no viable education or skills, she saw an ad in a local newspaper, "Adult entertainment, make $2,000 a week." It was an ad for a brothel. It was licensed and appeared safe. The reality she experienced was indignity and trauma from being bought for sexual use over 4,300 times. It only took a few months before Andrea had a severe mental breakdown. She told herself prostitution was a job like any other. She identified as a sex worker, which for her, became an act of self-preservation.

At twenty-five years of age Andrea built a licensed brothel of her own, convinced that better working conditions would make it safe. That decision revealed to her that the real source of the harm is the men who buy sex. She had been under the illusion that she held power when in fact it was the misogynistic, sexually charged and entitled men who had the power and used it to choke, slap, bite, spit, verbally abuse, secretly film, stalk her, and more. Her conclusion is that commercial sex is a patriarchal system of thinly veiled rape that affords men the opportunity to use money rather than physical force to meet their demands for immediate sexual gratification. It is a continuum of harm and entails the objectification of women.

The conclusion one comes to from the experiences of these survivors is that no aspect of prostitution is safe. Behind closed doors there is violence without opportunity for interference. There is no access to help. No one cares for the victim. Prostitution is violence against women. There is no such thing as safe prostitution. Free or forced prostitution is the same industry. It is all violent and dangerous. Because there is so much money involved, prostitution is associated with a world of organized crime.

Prostitution is multi-traumatic and is not work. It is an atrocity to use the term work where women are beaten, sat on until they cannot breathe, forcibly impregnated, raped, gang-raped, raped with a weapon, anally raped, nearly drowned in a tub or toilet, choked, suffocated, porn photos taken, porn/snuff films made, forced to watch others harmed, threatened to be killed, and the list goes on and on. No buyer of sex cares if a prostitute is injured, trafficked, is under-age, or on drugs. The buyers only want that they want.

On December 20, 2013 an article in *National Post* by Barbara Kay was titled "Supreme Court falls for fairy tale that prostitutes are 'happy hookers' and not victims." The reality in prostitution is that great harm is caused to women and girls.

In the 2020 book *Souled Out* by Tania Filloleau,[17] she explains what prostitution is really like. She ran several brothels and up to 500 prostituted women worked for her. "Not a single one of these women said that she did not regret it." Many of her former employees became homeless, hopelessly drug-addicted, were murdered, or committed suicide. Most of these same women would have moved heaven and earth to prevent their own daughters from taking up such a life.

A survivor who spoke at a NCOSE (National Center on Sexual Exploitation) hosted conference encourages survivors to become thrivers and make change in the world. She suggests these steps to survive and thrive:

- Get support.
- Become hopeful.
- Know yourself.
- Have tools to heal.
- Help others heal.
- Become a change-maker.
- Have clear concrete boundaries.
- Communicate better with loved ones.
- Stand up for your community.
- Be a leader at home, at work.
- Know how to handle triggering situations.
- Own your voice.

"I wish I had been told these things when I was a young teenager: every human being has value and importance. We are not here to be used and abused, but to be loved, understood, and connected with. Trust your instincts and be on guard especially with any kind of romantic relationship opportunities. The right person will respect and honour you for all parts of who you are and not pressure you into anything.

It is okay to be curious about sexuality and that is normal and there are healthy and safe ways to learn about it. There are consequences of premarital sex and there is blessing that comes for waiting until marriage. Know what healthy relationships look like and the red flags in unhealthy relationships.

Watch out for job opportunities that are big money makers and sound too good to be true. Know what a healthy work environment looks like: your body is respected and not "sold." The employer will value you and treat you with respect. You are so much more than your body.

Sexuality is sacred and we must respect
ours and others' sexuality."

—A survivor

Endnotes

1 Protection of Communities and Exploited Persons Act. S.C. 2014, c.25 Assented to 2014-11-06. laws-lois.justice.gc.ca
2 Standing Committee on Justice and Human Rights, 41st Parliament. Consideration of Bill C-36, an Act to amend the Criminal Code. July 2014. ourcommons.ca
"Prostitution laws should follow Nordic Model, former sex trade worker says" CBC News, February 28, 2014. Testimonies of Natasha Falle, Casandra Diamond, Katarina McLeod, Linda and Ed Smith, Glendene Grant, Bridget Perrier, Marina Giacomin, Larissa Crack, Trisha Baptie, Timea Nagy.
3 Natasha Falle, founder of Sex Trade 101: Health Research Centre for the Study of Sexual Exploitation and Human Trafficking in Canada, University of Windsor. uwindsor.ca
4 Casandra Diamond, founder of BridgeNorth. bridgenorth.org
5 Katarina McLeod, founder of Rising Angels. risingangels.net
6 "Regina parents of slain women want tougher laws against johns" CBC News, December 20, 2013.
7 Glendene Grant, founder of Mothers Against Trafficking Humans (MATH), January 24, 2012.
8 "Human trafficking survivor says Indigenous women and girls especially at risk" by Rhiannon Johnson, CBC News, June 27, 2019.
9 "Should brothels be legal? Supreme Court of Canada ponders issue" by Julian Sher, Toronto Star, June 12, 2013.
10 "Childhood Trauma Linked to Chronic Diseases in Adulthood" by Vincent J. Felitti, Cancer InCytes, Volume 2, Issue 1, 2013. cancerincytes.org
11 "Marina Giacomin Speaks About Trafficking in Canada and Servants Anonymous" on youtube.com, May 22, 2013.
12 "Human Trafficking: Hidden in Alberta" by Alexandra Nicholson and Casandra Woods, Calgary Journal, August 24, 2017. calgaryjournal.ca
13 EVE, formerly Exploited Voices Now Educating. educating-voices.com
14 Timea Nagy. timeanagy.com
15 "Out of the Shadows" by Timea Nagy and Shannon Moroney, published 2019 by Penguin Random House Canada.
16 Standing Committee on Justice and Human Rights, 44th Parliament, 1st session, Number 007, March 22, 2022. Review of Protection of Communities and Exploited Persons Act. Testimony of Sex Trafficked Survivor Andrea Heinz. Her research articles can be found in the Dignity Journal at digitalcommons.uri.edu/dignity/vol5/iss1/8/
17 "Souled Out" by Tania Fiolleau, published by Micro Publishing Media, 2010. ISBN-10 1936517124

CHAPTER 12

Indigenous Women and Girls

"Indigenous women and girls are severely over-represented in the sex industry; this is the most egregious form of systemic racism in the country."

CATHY PETERS

*Statement to B.C. Indigenous Chiefs and
Federal Minister of Justice David Lametti, February 25, 2021*

It has been a privilege to meet and present to Indigenous groups around B.C. An Indigenous leader in B.C., MLA Ellis Ross, heard me present and he promptly spoke on a video about the harm prostitution causes to Indigenous women and girls. He was willing to raise awareness in his community.

Presenting at Missing and Murdered Indigenous Women and Girls (MMIWG) gatherings as a keynote speaker on three occasions has been another honour. The MMIWG inquiry is lengthy and is broad in scope addressing all forms of violence including sexual violence. It was worthwhile attending the sessions and breakout rooms where Indigenous women were open and candid about their experiences and trauma. They acknowledged that a healing strategy is needed because prostitution, trafficking, domestic violence, incest, and violence against women and girls have created a crisis point in the Indigenous communities.

Complex trauma or complex PTSD is a public health crisis and is pervasive in Indigenous communities. Complex trauma develops from a culmination of prolonged repetitive trauma events.[1] It is interpersonal involving harm and exploitation from primary caregivers during vulnerable times of life. Adverse Child Experiences[2] (ACE) create vulnerability and are:

- Abuse which can be emotional, sexual or physical.
- Neglect which can be physical and emotional.
- Household challenges, which include divorce, substance abuse, mental illness, domestic violence, and incarceration.

In addition, three main risk factors for human trafficking and sexual exploitation are:

- Past sexual abuse.
- Emotional neglect.
- Parent separation or loss.

These factors make children and youth vulnerable to be trafficked and will impact their development. Once they have been involved in the sex industry, the challenge is keeping them out. In order to heal and recover the following factors need to be addressed:

- Complex trauma and complex PTSD.
- Grief reactions.
- Chronic illness.
- Relationship stress.
- Addictions.

The problem is that many of the Indigenous communities, particularly those in the north, are isolated and remote. They are hard to get to and hard to get out of. Many Indigenous never leave their communities even though they know things are not working for them. They feel shame and therefore keep silent.

Along with presenting at MMIWG gatherings, there have been opportunities to present to Indigenous youth workers, Indigenous educators, to the House of the Moon empowerment project, and providing an information booth at the Assembly of First Nations convention in Vancouver. There was a great deal to learn from these experiences.

Indigenous women are seen as life-givers of society. Their hope is for more age-appropriate education on the issue of trafficking for their youth, more online help services and more drop-in centres. While friendship centres are a positive step, the problem is that anybody can drop in, including those who perpetrate danger and problems in the community. Women want rape kits and access to Indigenous forensic nurses, otherwise, victims are afraid to go for help.

Women in the communities often do not have a formal education, lack a positive male or father influence and did not receive love as they were growing up. These factors created vulnerability in their lives. The vulnerability was then taken advantage of by negative influencers inside the community and outside the community.

In the summer of 2022, the difficult R vs Alcorn[3] case in Manitoba received national attention. I was interviewed on Winnipeg radio and Global News TV in Manitoba by Marney Blunt. This was a particularly disturbing case because it involved an underage Indigenous girl who was sexually exploited, filmed, and later committed suicide. The perpetrator was charged and appealed for a lighter sentence. Instead, the justices quadrupled his sentence, which has set a court precedent for the whole country. It was encouraging to see the court taking this crime very seriously and deliver a higher sentence than expected.

By attending numerous Indigenous meetings including the MMIWG gatherings I heard the hope expressed that chiefs would put through calls for justice and address the violence and sexual assault in their communities. Keeping communities sober was identified as a common call. Suggestions and questions that were raised were:

- Healing must begin in each community by addressing trauma.
- Youth are tech savvy, so how can they be safe online?
- Can communities develop safety plans? With strategies and protocols?
- Traffickers are targeting boys to sell drugs and traffic girls. How can this be stopped?
- Mentorship is required for youth to keep them out of the drug and sex industry. Who can mentor?
- What healthy alternatives can be created for boys to make money? For girls to make money?
- There needs to be mental health services on par with those offered for physical health.
- Prevention programs that already exist could be incorporated: on substance abuse, anti-bullying, teen pregnancy, suicide prevention and now human trafficking and sexual exploitation. These prevention programs have a significant cost benefit for communities in the long term.
- What ways can our women and girls be honoured in a modern context?
- What is needed for Indigenous women and girls to feel safe?
- Can safe spaces be made available for Indigenous women and girls?
- Are there supports for reporting sexual crime?
- How can sexual crime be addressed in a culturally sensitive manner?

- How can women support each other, so that women will come forward and speak up?
- What are the unique vulnerabilities in our communities and how do we address these?
- What can Indigenous leaders, chiefs and elders do to effectively address this issue both within and without the community?
- How can the difficult issues be brought out in the open so there can be healing; issues such as childhood sexual assault and incest?
- How can we teach our men and boys to respect, honour and protect our women and girls?
- How can we encourage Indigenous men and boys to not hurt or be violent?
- How can alcohol and drug use be addressed in a proactive way so that it can be stopped?
- How can trafficking and pimping be addressed and stopped within our communities?
- How can the vulnerable be protected?
- How can families heal?
- How can Indigenous men and boys be reached with positive messaging about how to be good influencers and good role models?
- How can we warn about pornography viewing in Indigenous communities?
- How can our youth and children thrive and become resilient despite adversity and vulnerability?
- How can we address adverse childhood experiences so that our Indigenous youth have healthy childhoods and can grow up in healthy environments?
- How can we raise awareness about human trafficking with our youth and children, so they are not victimized?
- What are parenting strategies that work?

A positive Indigenous initiative that is having national impact is the Moosehide Campaign,[4] a grassroots movement of Indigenous and non-Indigenous men standing up against violence towards women and children. Paul Lacerte and his daughter Raven started this campaign in 2011. Their campaign was founded on the side of the Highway of Tears in response to the injustices and violence faced by too many women and children in Canada, particularly those who are Indigenous. There are four pillars to this campaign in which men and boys promise to:

- Stand up with women and children and speak out against violence towards them.
- Support each other as men and hold each other accountable.
- Teach young boys about the true meaning of love and respect and be healthy role models for them.
- Heal as men and support our brothers on their healing journey.

The campaign is identified by wearing a moose hide pin that signifies the commitment to honour, respect and protect the women and children in a man's life, with the goal to end gender-based violence and take action towards reconciliation with Indigenous peoples. According to the Moosehide Campaign website, half of all women in Canada have experienced at least one incident of violence by the age of sixteen. It is worse for Indigenous women.

Dr. Martin Brokenleg[5] from Victoria addresses how to raise Indigenous youth using traditional practices. He uses a model of leadership that identifies six areas of human need to meet full potential: safety, belonging, achievement, power, purpose, and adventure.

Two parenting practices that are useful to prevent sexual exploitation are to teach emotional resilience, and create secure attachment.[6]

Teaching emotional resilience is done when children know they are safe and can talk about their concerns. Children need to feel nurtured and noticed when they're growing up. Parents have significant influence and can model and teach healthy emotional coping skills so youth can cope with stress and adversity and learn to meet challenges head on. How is this done?

- Allow children to make mistakes and learn natural consequences for their behaviour.
- Use empathy and express confidence in them.
- Help children to identify and cope with their emotions.
- Role model resiliency: children are sponges; they watch, learn and copy.
- Have children be accountable for their actions. Set boundaries and continue.
- Teach them to express what they are feeling.

Secure attachment is about creating a safe haven and a secure base so that this foundation carries over to future relationships. How is this done? Have a loving routine in the home, parents attending their children's games and events, spending quality time together and doing special activities. Allow youth to express their emotions. Be available, responsive and engaged. Parenting is a sacred space. It is preventative, proactive and loving. Youth and children want to know they do not need to navigate life alone. There are healthy strategies for planning for the future. They need to learn to:

- Develop healthy interpersonal communication skills.
- Know the difference between healthy versus unhealthy relationships (refer to Cybertip.ca under the Education and Resources section, "It is a BIG deal").
- Understand the benefits of abstinence from drugs, alcohol, and sex because alcohol and drugs play significant roles in sexual assaults against teens.

- Maintain reproductive health.
- Understand good nutrition.
- Understand risk reduction behaviours to themselves and others.
- Understand the importance of personal responsibility and boundaries.
- Understand relationships with others.
- Learn effective communication skills.
- Use critical thinking skills to understand situations and make appropriate decisions.
- Understand the importance of goals.
- Develop healthy coping strategies.
- Know where to find resources for help, mentorship within and without the community.

Endnotes

1   "Complex PTSD: Post-Traumatic Stress Disorder" National Health Service, United Kingdom. nhs.uk
2   "What are ACEs? And how do they relate to Toxic Stress?" ACEs: Center on the Developing Child, Harvard University. developingchild.harvard.edu Adverse Childhood Experiences Study: cdc.gov/violenceprevention/childabuseandneglect/acestudy/
3   "Manitoba appeals court gives harsher sentence in 'precedent-setting' sex trafficking case" by Elisha Dacey, Global News, December 15, 2021. Known as R vs Alcorn, Manitoba Court of Appeal overturned the sentence of a Winnipeg man convicted of sexually exploiting an Indigenous underaged girl.
4   Moosehide Campaign. moosehidecampaign.ca
5   Martin Brokenleg. martinbrokenleg.com
6   "Prevent Porn Problems With Two Parenting Practices: Teaching Emotional Resilience and Creating Secure Attachment" by Amanda Christensen, September 14, 2021. hopemft.com

CHAPTER 13

Missing and Murdered Indigenous Women and Girls

"Injustice anywhere is a threat to justice everywhere."

MARTIN LUTHER KING JR.

It was a privilege to meet Chief Commissioner Marion Buller[1] of Missing and Murdered Indigenous Women and Girls (MMIWG) at the University Women's Club in Vancouver. We had ongoing conversations in person and by email.

Marion encouraged me to read the June 2019 MMIWG final report[2] in which she was part of a huge research team. The title of the report is "Reclaiming power and place: the way to end violence is to restore women and girls to their rightful place in the communities." Two-thousand-four-hundred people across Canada were heard. There were two-hundred-thirty-one recommendations or calls for justice.

The question is, "How many Indigenous women and girls have gone missing and been murdered?" There was an inability to classify the investigations. But what struck Marion was the diversity of Indigenous people across the country. It is a rich and diverse heritage environmentally, culturally and in language. Sadly, there was a huge breach of human rights and the harm to Indigenous women and girls is

88

deliberate and ongoing. The context for Indigenous women and girls is pervasive trauma, poverty and abuse.

Another question is, "What can be done to reduce the violence?" There must be acknowledgement that violence is occurring. A goal is for peaceful and respectful homes. Setting ground rules within families was cited as a way to move forward in a positive way. For example, some families agree on rules in their homes: no swearing, no violence, no gang insignia, no weapons, no drugs, and no alcohol. For some there are consequences by family members if these rules are breeched. Some families have no rules, and some individuals will not change so the community must speak out. The youth need to be engaged. Substance abuse is a concern. One family moved forward in a healthy way; all three generations went to drug treatment professionals.

Residential school victims are more understood today, and families are reconciling because they are talking out in the open. A conclusion was that what individuals learn at home is what they carry forward in their lives. If violence is not tolerated at home, everyone can learn to move forward. Some of the other questions asked:

- What sort of community do we want to live in?
- What future do we want for our families and communities?
- How do we keep our people safe?
- In the larger context, who is at the decision-making tables and boards?

There is a consensus that there must be zero tolerance of violence in the home, in the schools, and in the community with the goal to thrive and be healthy.

Men and women need to be educated and treated as equal partners. Men need to look out for the safety of the women in their communities.

As an example, the Moosehide Campaign has begun the conversation in some communities.

Marion pointed out that MMIWG testimonies can be watched online. One testimony that stood out to me was by Diane Redsky[3] (Executive Director, MaMawi Wi Chi Itata Centre and Project Director, National Task Force on Human Trafficking of Women and Girls in Canada, 2011–2015) from Manitoba. This is what Diane said about the business of sex trafficking:

> "The situation of sex trafficking and sexual exploitation in Canada is getting worse. It is a growing problem that is almost out of control. There is a specific target and market for young very vulnerable Indigenous girls. When I started doing this work twenty-five years ago the average age of recruitment was thirteen years of age, and now it is getting much younger. The perpetrators are posing as boyfriends, managers or friends, sometimes even peers. So, it is harder to figure out who is that bad friend or bad boyfriend. Trafficking and sexual exploitation is becoming less visible because it is going online. The internet is making it possible, as one mother put it, 'to enter my daughter's bedroom through her computer screen.' Sex trafficking is getting more profitable for more people. The big problem is the lack of money available for the people on the front lines doing the hard work. National coordination is missing. This crime does not recognize borders. There needs to be national oversight."

At a Federal Justice Committee an Indigenous elder spoke up to say that the MMIWG inquiry did not address prostitution. She stated that prostitution is a plague to aboriginal women and exacerbates homelessness, vulnerability and violence. Indigenous women cannot expose or break the silence regarding the extensive male violence. Yet voices are saying prostitution is viable work. She ended by saying there are no options for indigenous women and prostitution is a highway to hell.

At the MMIWG gatherings there were Indigenous speakers that shared their stories. They were personal, painful and poignant. One woman, who has become a trauma expert in mental health, has learned from her own painful past. Self-care is the starting place. Strong mentors and healthy choices everyday made a difference. Begin each day with gratitude and thoughts of success. It is important to drink water every day. She was often triggered by her trauma but gets herself into the present. It was difficult growing up with violence, where she was powerless and had no voice. People experiencing trauma, who have had no voice when they are young, may start to talk too much as they get older. She warned that too much talk could be a coping mechanism. "Pay attention if there is too much talk." Covid-19 is a challenge for every community and the isolation is difficult because the Indigenous are relational and community centered.

Another speaker talked of the necessity of cultivating resiliency in her life after sexual trauma. She learned that body awareness is important because trauma causes detachment from the body. "Our stories are held in our bodies." To reclaim safety in her life she needed to learn to communicate and find positive support systems. Fear is deep. When fear is triggered, she found it would quickly spiral downward. She needed to be told, "You are okay." Just a phone call from a friend helped her.

It was difficult processing her emotions because she had experienced compound trauma in her life. She became an alcoholic. Being in the arms of her mother and grandmother helped her and she learned she needed to be a strong sober mother for her son. She had to learn how to ask for support. Indigenous women will typically carry loads alone. It was important for her to figure out her triggers. Learning boundaries and how to express those boundaries to others became an ongoing priority.

She recognized her trauma could unwind her very quickly. However, she has learned there is a healing journey. When she speaks, she talks about alcohol. Alcohol use is a problem for her and her friends; many of them could not stop drinking. It was non-stop drinking all day, until they passed out. Chronic alcohol use puts women in vulnerable and dangerous situations for abuse, rape and violence. She got to a point in her life where she could not stay sober. At one point she called a friend and told her what was happening; then many messages were sent to her from more friends to give her hope. All these messages gave her enough hope to choose life and change her lifestyle.

Another woman experienced an abusive relationship for years and she had four children with the man who abused her. The abuse she experienced began at the beginning of the relationship, yet it took her years to realize what was happening and to finally leave. She believed the lies, and believed she was nothing, stupid, and not trustworthy. When she left him she was expecting her fourth child. What helped her was knowing she belonged to aunties and cousins. She took parenting courses. Those courses helped. Her mother and father helped her to talk and to stay strong.

She was motivated to have a good life and safe home for her children. Her key was to stay connected with her family. Her grandmother was a particularly strong role model who had not gone to residential school. Through all her years she was loved through it all.

She signed up for college and took counselling courses so she could understand family violence. She learned that compassion, care and understanding are needed in relationships. Leaving her husband was very hard and she felt mom guilt. Leaving was necessary because she had become a shell of a person.

Another woman shared that both her parents had attended residential school. Her parents had six children. She felt worthless at a very young age. Neglect and abandonment were all she knew, and she knew she was not loved or wanted. She met her husband through her mother. She ignored the red flags of this relationship, and that he had just gotten out of jail. She was determined to tough it out and stay married, although her husband beat her regularly for years. She lived with chronic head injuries and was unable to make decisions. She was clinically depressed, had ulcers and her body held all the pain.

She did not know what to do. It was her children that saved her. So, she went to school and was motivated to mother her children. Everything in her community was linked around alcohol, but she and her husband did not drink. This was not enough however to stop the chaos in their family life. She fought back. Her advice: address any head injuries and find consistent loving connectedness. Stay connected with loving healthy people.

Another woman shared her story. She was married for years to an abusive husband. She finally left him. Her call is for men's groups. She believes men's groups are desperately needed today. Her question, "How do we have conversations with men and boys? Their role is supposed to be to protect women and girls in their families."

Other women suggested grandmother groups so that the older women would mentor the younger Indigenous women in their communities.

One woman complained that reservations and communities in Canada and the USA are recruitment centres for the sex industry and for traffickers. She felt that the mothers and grandmothers have no idea the pressure put on the young girls. Drugs are sold to the youth, and they end up with drug debts they have to pay off. Organized crime is involved with the drug trade and with human sex trafficking. Drugs come into the communities and the girls are sex trafficked out of the communities. Young native women go missing and no one cares. There are runaways from the foster care system because there is no sense of safety or security. The shadow pandemic is violence against women.

Many women shared that there needs to be awareness about internet safety. Stranger danger is not understood because online everyone is a "friend."

The consensus was that Indigenous women and girls must develop resiliency to survive sexual violence and it is important to regain their voice and strength.[4] They all admitted it is hard work to "find ourselves as an Indian woman, to own and love and to take care of our bodies and revive our spirits." Everyone was encouraged to think of the strongest person in their family to find a mentor, then to be a mentor.

B.C. has a First Nations Health Authority, which is the first of its kind in Canada. There will be helpful resources through the authority.

House of the Moon is an Indigenous empowerment program that is grassroots. The goal of the program is to find solutions and make it easy for people to come together. There are scholarships and fundraising. The hope is to help Indigenous women understand where they have come from to support and mentor the next generation.

Some Indigenous leaders mentioned that cash handouts are not necessarily the best thing for the bands. Extra money is used for drugs and alcohol harming the communities even more. People in many communities drink longer and may drink continually. Many felt that the monies from the government should be used for programs that show a better healthy way.

Endnotes

1   Marion Buller, Chief Commissioner of MMIWG. mmiwg-ffada.ca
2   "Reclaiming Power and Place: The Final Report of the National Inquiry into Missing and Murdered Indigenous Women and Girls" The National Inquiry's Final Report. mmiwg-ffada.ca/final-report/
    "The Business of Sex Trafficking" by Diane Redsky. mmiwg-ffada.ca/video-clips
3   "Diane Redsky wins Governor General's Award for work with Indigenous Women" CBC News, November 10, 2016.
4   "MMIWG Memorial Unveiled Along B.C.'s Highway of Tears" by Courtney Dickson, Kate Partridge. CBC News, September 12, 2022. Dozens of family members and friends turned out for Sunday unveiling of 'Journey of Hope' monument.

CHAPTER 14

British Columbia

"Splendour without diminishment."

The British Columbia motto referring to the sun on the shield,
which although setting, never decreases.

British Columbia is the westernmost province in Canada, bordering on the Pacific Ocean. It is internationally known for its stunning natural beauty. The Vancouver area is the most heavily populated in B.C. and has become particularly vulnerable to trafficking as a port city, an entry point into Canada and close to the US border.

Initially the focus for my work was B.C. where we live. My goal is to raise awareness about this crime to stop it with a focus on child sex trafficking. It is youth and children who are being aggressively targeted, exploited and harmed by the sex industry.

Presenting to all levels of government—civic, provincial and federal— as well as to law enforcement was first steps. Then, in addition, I was asked to present to more groups including frontline service providers, health professionals, school boards, police boards, universities, high schools, and service clubs. It has been surprising to find that there is a general lack of awareness about this crime. In particular, the public do not understand the serious implications of the potential of full decriminalization of prostitution in Canada if the PCEPA law was to be repealed. A repealed law would mean that sex traffickers and sex buyers would be able to act with impunity. My advocacy work has focused on "connecting the dots" so the public understands the crime and can report it in order to prevent it.

The Protection of Communities and Exploited Persons Act (PCEPA), which became Federal Law in 2014, is not purposely enforced in British Columbia according to the B.C. Law Enforcement Guidelines. As mentioned in previous chapters the law criminalizes the sex buyer and profiteer because they are the root cause of sexual exploitation. While police in B.C. lack training in human trafficking, they know human trafficking and sexual exploitation is a problem and law enforcement is receptive to learning more about the crime.

Alberta, Manitoba (with Joy Smith), Ontario and Nova Scotia[1] have best practices with law enforcement and prevention education. Also, there has been excellent media coverage in these provinces on the crime (see Globe and Mail journalists Tavia Grant and Robyn Doolittle),[2] whereas there has been virtually no media coverage in B.C. As a result, B.C. is far behind in addressing awareness of sex trafficking and sexual exploitation. B.C. has similarities to Washington State regarding a sharp increase in crime, drug use, prostitution and human trafficking. Watch the *Seattle Is Dying* and the newly released *Vancouver Is Dying* documentaries.[3]

My question for law enforcement and politicians is, "How many johns or sex buyers have you charged?" Except for the effective john stings in Vancouver in 2019, the province has focused on charging only a few notorious traffickers.[4] Charging the traffickers will not stop the crime. Going after the buyers, the root cause of exploitation is the only way to stop the crime.

Valiant Richey, who is a global expert with the OSCE, has written a report called *Discourage Demand*,[5] which is a timely report to the global community on what is needed to stop human trafficking. Valiant Richey states that trafficking has become an out-of-control global problem and we are losing in a very big way. Until countries address the demand for commercially paid sex, trafficking will continue to skyrocket. Trafficking will never be stopped because there is a great deal of money involved.

Numerous high-profile cases have occurred in British Columbia, but charges remain low. Here, the Crown Counsel is responsible for making charges. By contrast in Ontario police can make charges directly. Having this extra layer to make prosecutions in B.C. means the Crown Counsel must have the will to prosecute the crime. Currently this province is short on investigations and prosecutions. As gang presence and activity increases in B.C., the sex industry is able to grow, and this undermines community safety.

More counter exploitation or sex crime units are needed in every jurisdiction. The Vancouver Police Department has the most experienced, trained and largest counter exploitation unit in the province. Police need to be proactive in addressing this crime, yet with inadequate funding, this is not happening. Officers need to be highly trained and tech crime specialists are needed because this crime is occurring online. Banks, to track money-laundering, and cell phone companies also have a part to play in addressing this crime and can be complicit if they do not have the training to recognize the red flags.

Sexual exploitation in B.C. was international headline news during the trial of Robert Pickton,[6] Canada's most infamous, brutal serial killer who targeted prostituted women. He murdered dozens of women, many of which were Indigenous women from Vancouver's Downtown Eastside. As Brian McConaghy described in his testimony to Parliament (Chapter 5), Robert Pickton represents the brutal and deadly reality of the sex industry. The book, *That Lonely Section of Hell* by Lorimer Shenher[7] describes the investigation of this serial killer who almost got away. I encourage law enforcement to read this book and I remind politicians and the public that this type of case must never happen again.

Most victims of prostitution end up drug addicted, mentally ill, committing suicide or are murdered—only about 5% get out of the sex industry. The cost to rehabilitate survivors according to Joy Smith is well over $60,000 per year for at least eight years; although victims never really ever get over the trauma because of the complex PTSD they suffer.

Reza Moazami is Canada's most prolific sex trafficker. He was given the longest jail time to date for trafficking at least twenty individuals, many of them underage. His sentence is twenty-three years in jail. He was masterful and extremely manipulative with his victims.

It is worth reading the CANLII R. v. Moazami 2014 report. The Honourable Madam Justice Bruce presided over this gruesome case and found Moazami guilty of thirty out of thirty-six charges including sexual exploitation, sexual assault and living off the avails of prostitution. While crown prosecutors asked for a twenty-year sentence, Judge Bruce sentenced Moazami to twenty-three years in prison. Moazami was charged for eleven victims who ranged in age from fourteen to nineteen. Most of the victims were sexually exploited children. Many were drug addicted, homeless, with developmental delays or were runaways who had experienced a lot of violence. His case was the first human trafficking conviction in the province. Moazami comes from North Vancouver, and in his mid-twenties lured local, vulnerable girls on Facebook by promising them drugs, alcohol and in one instance, a puppy. Moazami sought an appeal in June 2022, but the Supreme Court dismissed his appeals.[8]

Human trafficking for the purpose of prostitution is a powerful and rapidly growing enterprise. Human trafficking cases are not isolated incidences that occur infrequently. We must all be alert to signs of trafficking in our jurisdictions and aggressively follow the smallest clue. That was how Reza Moazami was caught. A teacher noticed a difference in her student's dress and demeanour and reported it. Sex trafficking can happen anywhere, however unlikely a place. Investigators need to be aware of and recognize the signs of trafficking (Chapter 10).

Michael Bannon[9] is a Vancouver sex trafficker who ran an underage prostitution ring. He pleaded guilty to twenty-two charges based on the evidence of eight victims. This trafficker also used the internet to lure his victims contacting them through Facebook. He promised large financial rewards. In turn he placed the sex ads for his victims online. Bannon was out on parole for previous crimes when he began putting together the highly lucrative Vancouver prostitution ring that eventually landed him with his fourteen-year sentence. He also has a lifetime ban from accessing the internet.

B.C. is notorious for the Highway of Tears, a 725-kilometre corridor of Highway 16 between Prince George and Prince Rupert. It has been the location of many MMIWG since 1970.[10]

MMIWG gatherings have been an important avenue for Indigenous women and girls to address issues of violence and reclaim their power and place by sharing and gathering their stories from as many as possible to build a strong foundation for healing, justice and reconciliation. I had the honour of presenting at three gatherings and these gave me wonderful opportunities to hear stories and make friends.

One of the first books written on human trafficking in Canada was *Invisible Chains* by UBC law professor Benjamin Perrin.[11] He is a leading researcher on human trafficking in Canada and advised the federal government on the issue. It is the first book to describe the national phenomenon of human trafficking in Canada, with excellent documentation and research. Perrin discovered there are a lot more victims in Canada than the public is aware of. Joy Smith calls it the hidden crime of human trafficking, Canada's secret shame and produced a documentary with that title, *Human Trafficking, Canada's Secret Shame* (Appendix G: Resources).

Benjamin Perrin went on to write the book *Victim Law* for legal professionals in Canada. At his book presentation at UBC he highlighted his research showing that in Canada there are 2.2 million victims of serious crimes each year with aboriginal women disproportionately represented. He reports that 95% of sexual assaults go unreported. Why? There is fear of retaliation, little trust in the police, privacy violations and a crisis of confidence, so victims are not willing to report.

Perrin encourages and supports the principles and pillars of victim law where there is the right to information for the victim, protection for the victims, participation in the process of restorative justice, reparations (victim compensation) and remedies for victims. He has encouraged provinces and territories to train police, crown prosecutors and judges to enforce restitution and to expand restoration justice laws. He lists Timea Nagy (Chapter 11) and former NHL hockey player Sheldon Kennedy (Chapter 15) as vocal survivors who have shared their stories and trauma so that more victims would be encouraged to come forward and report.

The most infamous case of a B.C. girl that gave a face to human trafficking is Jessie Foster[12] mentioned in Chapter 11. She was a young woman from Kamloops, British Columbia who met a man at a party and agreed to travel with him to Florida. Jessie ended up in Las Vegas where she was sold through escort ads. Her mother Glendene Grant has spent years looking for her daughter who went missing at twenty-one years of age. Jessie's case has been profiled on *America's Most Wanted* list along with other women who have vanished in Las Vegas' seedy underworld. Survivor Timea Nagy features Jessie Foster in her music video called "Break the Silence" (Canadian version).

British Columbia needs a province-wide strategy to stop human trafficking combined with well-trained, compassionate and well-funded law enforcement. Public awareness is being done ad hoc across B.C.

Law enforcement officers tell me that Surrey and Vancouver are known as Canada's pimp playground and that B.C. is attracting criminals from the rest of Canada. Why? B.C. is not charging these criminals, particularly repeat offenders.

There needs to be engagement with Indigenous communities and with new Canadians who come to Canada as migrants. It is critical to engage with new Canadians because there are different norms of behaviour between the sexes in other countries, and they need to be aware of this country's laws.

Cultural isolation needs to be addressed, as new migrants settle into communities. There needs to be better collaboration throughout the province to address the "silo mentalities" that accomplish little overall. Including these newcomers into the communities would be of value.

British Columbia has the Office to Combat Trafficking in Persons (OCTIP) and VictimLink BC with a provincial helpline for B.C. and the Yukon (1-800-563-0808 text or call).[13] VictimLink BC provides information and referral services to all victims of crime and immediate crisis support to victims of family and sexual violence including victims of human trafficking exploited for labour or sexual services. The problem is neither agency is well advertised. Crown counsels need training and the attorney general needs to be supportive. Media needs to report on this crime rather than publicize support for the rights of the pro-prostitution lobby and sex industry. The public needs to be aware and engaged.

For prevention of human sex trafficking, the Children of the Street has a significant reach in schools in B.C. by doing role-play presentations to grades three to twelve, and reach up to 25,000 students per year. Tiana Sharifi used to work for Children of the Street and has founded SEE, Sexual Exploitation Education. She understands the role of social media in human trafficking and the sex industry, has participated in ground-breaking research and presents in B.C. and nationally.[14]

Exiting services are needed in B.C. The Salvation Army operates the effective 24/7 wrap around program called Deborah's Gate.[15] Covenant House offers services for underage trafficked youth. The stages of service that are needed are:

- Emergency care: detox, food, shelter, safety.
- Stabilization.
- Re-integration into society.
- Transition. The biggest gap in the services provided in B.C. and in Canada is first stage programs and detox.

VCASE, the Vancouver Collective Against Sexual Exploitation is a non-partisan group of diverse individuals and organizations that have come together as a single voice to end all forms of sexual exploitation.[16] There is an impressive breadth of life experience of the men and women who attend. Several women in the group presented at the February 2022 Federal Justice Committee on the review of PCEPA. VCASE consists of several survivors of prostitution as well as prevention educators, researchers, writers, and professionals of all kinds. Their website has excellent video vignettes, a research section and template letters for citizens to write to politicians and police. While the Vancouver area has a robust sex industry, it is encouraging that a collective like VCASE has been formed to counter sexual exploitation in the Lower Mainland. To summarize, in B.C. there needs to be:

- Provincial educational campaign.
- Updating of provincial police policies.
- Education for crown counsel and judiciary.
- School education.

Specifically, there needs to be regional workshops, meetings with other jurisdictions, law enforcement collaboration (no silos), available victim services, NGO involvement, facilitation and development of networks, sharing of best practices with the goal to participate in a national initiative that addresses human trafficking.

Endnotes

1   "The Reading Stone: The Survivor's Lens to Human Trafficking" Alberta's Human Trafficking Action Plan, August 31, 2021. Alberta Task Force. alberta.ca
    "Responding to Sexual Exploitation: Tracia's Trust" Manitoba. gov.mb.ca
    "Ontario's anti-human trafficking strategy 2020–2025" Ontario. ontario.ca
    "Provincial Approach to Address Human Trafficking, Sexual Exploitation" Nova Scotia. novascotia.ca
2   "The Trafficked: The story behind our investigation into the exploitation of Indigenous women and girls" by Tavia Grant, Globe and Mail, February 10, 2016. theglobeandmail.com
    "Unfounded: Police dismiss 1 in 5 sexual assaults claims as baseless" by Robyn Doolittle, Globe and Mail, February 3, 2017. theglobeandmail.com
3   "Seattle is Dying" by Eric Johnson, Komo News Special, March 14, 2019. youtube.com
    "Vancouver is Dying" by Aaron Gunn, October 5, 2022. youtube.com
4   "47 men arrested by Vancouver police operation targeting alleged sexual predators" by Rhianna Schmunk, CBC, January 23, 2019.
5   "Discouraging the Demand that fosters trafficking for the purpose of sexual exploitation" OSCE, June 10, 2021. osce.org
6   "It has been 20 years since police raided Robert Pickton's B.C. pig farm" by Amy Judd, Global News, February 7, 2022. The pig farm property became the site of the largest crime scene search in the country's history. Pickton was charged for 26 murders connected with the disappearances of dozens of women from Vancouver's Downtown Eastside.
7   "That Lonely Section of Hell" by Lorimer Shenher, Greystone Books, 2015.
8   "Supreme Court of Canada will not hear appeal by convicted B.C. sex trafficker" by the Canadian Press, CBC News, British Columbia, June 30, 2022. Canada's highest court will not hear an appeal from Reza Moazami, who was sentenced to 23 years in prison for trafficking 11 female victims, including underage girls, for sex.

9 "Michael Bannon gets lifetime ban and prison term for underage prostitution ring" by Bethany Lindsey, CBC News, February 14, 2018. cbc.ca

10 Symposium and Recommendations Report. highwayoftears.org

11 "Invisible Chains" by Benjamin Perrin, Viking Press, 2010. The first comprehensive book on human trafficking in Canada.

12 "Kamloops mom marks 16th anniversary of daughter lost to human trafficking" by Shannon Ainslie, infonews.ca, March 24, 2022. Glendene Grant started an organization called Mothers Against Trafficking Humans and speaks about human trafficking. She is an advocate for missing women and helps people understand how human trafficking works. In 2014, Grant got Jessie's Law passed, making it illegal to purchase or advertise sexual services and illegal to live on the material benefits from sex work in Canada.

13 VictimLink B.C., Province of B.C. www2.gov.bc.ca

14 Tiana Sharifi with SEE, Sexual Exploitation Education: "40% of online escort ads in B.C. suggest child trafficking: Study" by Nathan Griffiths, Vancouver Sun, July 16, 2022. "This is research-based proof and evidence that human trafficking is prevalent in our province, and that human trafficked victims are bought and sold in the same industry as sex workers," Tiana Sharifi, CEO of SEE, said in a statement. "Sextortion truths laid bare for teens, parents in North Van talks" by Jane Seyd, North Shore News, November 22, 2022. Cyber safety presenter Tiana Sharifi talks to Grade 9 and Grade 10 students on the dangers of online sexual exploitation.

15 Salvation Army Illuminate. illuminateht.com

16 VCASE. vcase.ca

CHAPTER 15

Canada

"Canada is free,
and freedom is its nationality."

SIR WILFRED LAURIER
Canada's 7th Prime Minister

"Deep in our history of struggle for
freedom, Canada was the North Star."

MARTIN LUTHER KING, JR.

While my advocacy work is focused on British Columbia, my work applies nationally. One of my first steps was to contact every Member of Parliament in Canada, every senator and every premier. To every Member of Parliament, I sent packages and letters to inform them of the issue and problem. I sent emails to every senator and emails and packages to every premier. I received positive responses from many of them.

To understand this crime, the US State Department writes the Trafficking in Persons Report or TIP[1] every year where many of the countries in the world are assessed for their work on addressing human trafficking. The report on Canada is specific and cites gaps that need to be addressed. While Canada is ranked a Tier One country (most compliant to the minimum standards in the TIP report; see Chapter 24) in addressing human trafficking, the TIP report noted that Canada has improvements to make and issues to address.

For example, the following gaps in Canada are listed: lack of data collection, lack of victim services, poor collaboration between provincial and federal governments, the need for pro-active law enforcement, a growing number of Canadian child sex tourists, lack of training for prosecutors and judges, especially for the restitution for victims, the need to partner with private sector and financial institutions to look for money laundering as a consequence of the proceeds of crime. The TIP report is also clear on the most at-risk populations: Indigenous in particular, followed by migrants, LGBTQ2, the disabled, at-risk runaway youth and youth in the child welfare system.

A significant contributor to the crime in Canada is Pornhub (under the company name of Mindgeek) located in Montreal. Shockingly, it produces the majority of the world's free-to-view pornography. USA Pulitzer Prize winner and columnist Nicholas Kristoff in his article in the *New York Times*, December 4, 2020:"The Children of Pornhub, why does Canada allow this company to profit off videos of exploitation and assault?" exposed this situation. He states:

> *"Pornhub attracts 3.5 billion visits a month, more than Netflix, Yahoo or Amazon. Pornhub rakes in money from almost three billion ad impressions a day. One ranking lists Pornhub as the tenth most visited website in the world... Its site is infested with rape videos... I asked the National Center for Missing & Exploited Children to compile the number of images, videos and other content related to child sexual exploitation reported to it each year. In 2015, it received reports of 6.5 million videos; in 2017, 20.6 million; and in 2019, 69.2 million... Pornhub was the technology company with the third greatest impact on*

> *society in the 21st century, after Facebook and Google, but ahead of Microsoft, Apple and Amazon... with Pornhub, we have Jeffrey Epstein times 1,000."*

As a consequence, Quebec Senator Julie Miville-Dechene called for a restriction on the consumption of online pornography by young people through new federal legislation that would force porn sites to verify the ages of all users. Miville-Dechene wants to protect youth and children from porn that is shown so widely on these websites.[2]

While there have been prominent names in the USA associated with sexual exploitation such as Harvey Weinstein, Jeffrey Epstein, Dr. Larry Nassar, an individual that appeared in Canadian news recently is fashion designer Peter Nygard.[3] Peter Nygard faced sex trafficking and racketeering charges in the USA and multiple sexual assault charges in Canada. Two prominent victims of sexual assault are NHL hockey players Sheldon Kennedy[4] and Theo Fleury.[5] "Swift Current" is a documentary that explores the trauma and long road to recovery of Sheldon Kennedy who was sexually assaulted by his former junior hockey coach Graham James. Both Sheldon and Theo are powerful examples of boys who were sexually abused and that abuse was unspeakably harmful to them.

There are three national organizations involved in addressing human trafficking in Canada. While Federal Public Safety and the RCMP have sections addressing human trafficking, the Canadian Centre to End Human Trafficking, the Canadian Centre for the Protection of Children, and the National Centre of Human Trafficking Education have proactive national reach.

The Canadian Centre to End Human Trafficking (CCTEHT) in Ottawa operates the Canadian Human Trafficking Hotline Number at 1-833-900-1010.[6] They offer a 24/7 service in multiple languages anywhere in Canada. This agency connects victims and survivors to law enforcement, emergency shelters, transition housing, long-term supports, counsellors, and other trauma-informed services.

The CCTEHT released their first report on trends in human trafficking across Canada. The biggest problems are:

• Canadians are not aware of this crime.
• They do not believe it happens in Canada.
• They do not know the indicators of human trafficking.

The report found that the people most likely to report the crime and to help the victims are family members. At the same time, it can also be family members who traffic and sexually exploit their own children or grandchildren.

The Canadian Centre for the Protection of Children (C3P) out of Manitoba is a national charity operating for over thirty years and dedicated to the personal safety of all children.[7] Their goal is to reduce the sexual abuse and exploitation of children, assist in the location of missing children and prevent child victimization through several programs, services and resources. The C3P runs Cybertip.ca which is a centralized location for Canadians to report online child sexual exploitation. They also access education and prevention resources to help keep children safe online. This agency has grown into an international leader in child protection.

Of note is the research done by C3P that can be found on their website. For example, C3P released the most comprehensive study that has ever been done in Canada, on child sexual abuse by school personnel.[8] This data reveals the number and nature of sexual offences committed and allegedly committed against children by employees who are predominantly teachers within K to 12 schools across Canada between 1997 and 2017.

Of international significance, C3P owns and operates Project Arachnid,[9] which is an innovative victim-centric set of tools to combat the proliferation of Child Sexual Abuse Material (CSAM) or child pornography. It was launched in 2017 using technology to detect CSAM content at a rapid pace, offering a global solution for disrupting the distribution of this harmful material. Project Arachnid is a world leader in exposing the role that vast networks play in facilitating the spread of CSAM. Global hotlines and child protection organizations work with Project Arachnid to classify the material. As of November 1, 2022, they have processed 156 billion images, found 49 million suspected media while issuing 17 million takedown notices to host providers. The team will also assist individuals in contacting a host provider to request removal of images and videos.

The third national organization is the National Human Trafficking Education Centre based in Manitoba.[10] It is a unique online hub offering educational resources to help Canadians understand and fight human trafficking. The materials were developed by the Joy Smith Foundation and are available for a wide variety of audiences including youth, parents, educators, survivors, social workers, front line responders, medical professionals and those working in the justice system. Some of the courses are free and some are available for a fee.

To find sources, statistics and relevant information, there is Stats Canada, the Federal Public Safety website and National Child Exploitation Crime Centre (renamed from the National Human Trafficking Coordination Centre) under the RCMP. As of 2019 there is a national strategy to combat human trafficking under Public Safety Canada.

Historically Canada has been known for strong human rights, but it is very young in anti-human trafficking strategies. It is therefore critical to foster a culture of dignity in which all individuals in Canada are free from abuse and exploitation, and to incentivize men to change their views and attitudes towards the exploitation of women, children and the vulnerable.

Endnotes

1   Trafficking in Persons or TIP report, USA State Department. www.state.gov
2   "Senators vote to make platforms verify age of viewers to stop kids and teens accessing porn online" by Marie Woolf, The Globe and Mail, December 6, 2022. Senator Julie Miville-Dechene added a clause expanding the online streaming Bill C-11 to find ways to verify the age of people accessing pornography online.
3   "Canada orders Peter Nygard Extradited to U.S. once Canadian charges addressed" Reuters, US News, March 22, 2022.
4   "Trauma recovery of sex assault survivor Sheldon Kennedy" CBC, May 11, 2016.
5   "Theo Fleury was abused: Absolute nightmare, every day of my life" Maclean's, October 9, 2009.
6   Canadian Centre to End Human Trafficking. canadiancentretoendhumantrafficking.ca
7   Canadian Centre for Child Protection. protectchildren.ca
8   "Child Sexual Abuse by K-12 School Personnel in Canada: Executive Summary" is the most comprehensive study of child sexual abuse by school personnel ever done in Canada between 1997 and 2017. Canadian Centre for Child Protection. The published study is in the Journal of Child Sexual Abuse, published online June 12, 2018. doi.org
    A shocking statistic is that 86% of the perpetrators are certified teachers. "'Tip of the iceberg' Report finds 252 school personnel accused of sexual offences" The Canadian Press, CTV News, November 2, 2022.
9   Project Arachnid. projectarachnid.ca
10 "'We can hardly keep up': Education key to combat human trafficking experts say" by Brieanna Charlebois at the Canadian Press, National Post, October 30, 2021. Announcement of the launch of the National Human Trafficking Education Centre by the Joy Smith Foundation in Manitoba.

CHAPTER 16

The Internet

"Grooming is the tactic of overcoming the survivor's defenses by slowly desensitizing his or her natural reaction to abusive behaviours. Key protective factor: parents."

CORDELIA ANDERSON, PSYCHOLOGIST

Internet connection has been in our lives for over twenty years and has drastically changed our lives and how we inter-relate with one another. Today the internet is a gateway directly into the family home. The effects of the internet seem invisible. However, more than ever public and parental awareness of the insidious dark areas of the internet are needed. How can adults supervise the internet when the majority of children and youth have access to it? Parents must gain control of the internet in their own homes.

Charlene Doak-Gebauer has written the book *The Internet, Are Children In Charge?* and she presents tirelessly on this topic. Her concern is that the internet is facilitating more predation (sexual predators) than by any other means in the world. She recommends digital supervision training for adults and parents.[1] Children do not have the life experience to make good decisions online and predators are sophisticated with global reach. Abusers purposely seek out children and youth online.

Peer-to-peer victimizers have also increased. Sexting, or sharing nudes has become common, and is very dangerous. According to Doak-Gebauer one out of four teens receive sexts, one out of seven send sexts, and one out of ten forward sexts. A photo or sext can go through a school of one thousand students in one hour. The effects of sexting can be anxiety, depression, isolation, shame, and suicide. The Amanda Todd case in British Columbia is a glaring example of the dangers on the internet as mentioned in the previous chapter.

There are hidden epidemics online, for example child on child sexual assault has increased due to porn viewing. Child innocence is lost. Children can easily find pornography online, and the porn industry is aggressively seeking to get children and youth as young as six to eight years of age addicted. A predator online can trick a child simply by saying, "Let's do something silly or funny." Children can then become innocent victims of the internet.

Adults and parents must be organized with digital supervision. Having a digital contract with family members is a good start. The router can be kept in a locked place and turned off at night. Hard wire filters can be useful, although these can give a false sense of security.

Doek-Gebauer warns parents, that if they own the phone there are legal implications if their child sends nudes online as this is considered child pornography, which is illegal. She reminds parents, that if they are paying for a device, then it is important to monitor their child's activity online. This is not invasion of privacy but protecting self and children.

Two well-publicized cases involved Rehtaeh Parsons from Halifax and Amanda Todd from B.C.[2] Both girls give faces to cyber sex bullying. In 2011, Rehtaeh Parsons, a 15-year-old girl was raped at a party. The boys filmed and shared the video at school. In 2013, Rehtaeh killed herself. Amanda was a victim of sextortion and killed herself in 2012. The perpetrator from the Netherlands was finally charged and sentenced ten years later. Amanda's mother Carol has been tireless in exposing this crime publicly, very similar to Jessie Foster's mother, Glendene Grant.

According to the NGO Defend Young Minds[3] and Protect Young Eyes[4] we need empowered, resilient, tech-smart youth today. The exploitation of youth has become a big business. A dangerous trend is that the grooming process can happen in as few as eight days or less when youth are willing to meet with predators in person after meeting them online. Particularly during COVID-19, many youth were feeling isolated and depressed, bored and lonely. It is critical to know what children are doing online. The main vulnerability is the amount of time youth are online. The more time spent online, the increased vulnerability. Youth are switching to a virtual world, away from the real world.

Gaming is particularly concerning. Teenagers and young boys are being tricked into sending explicit pictures online.[5] What games are available online? Who are the children gaming with? How much time is spent gaming? Can gaming become addictive? A lot of gaming apps are designed to communicate with others, and this is where predators frequently hang out. Children as early as seven years of age are getting pulled into this sextortion. These new trends have occurred so fast that no one has been prepared for addressing them. Children seven to nine years old cannot understand the dangers and implications of being groomed. Trauma bonding occurs online, and these relationships become very difficult to break.

As children are preyed upon there are serious effects such as self-harm, cutting and suicidal thoughts. Children can also become predators themselves.[6] Pornography teaches youth to objectify themselves and to objectify others. Child-on-child sexual exploitation is a disturbing trend because children imitate what they view. Porn sexualizes children at a young age, which can cause them to act out sexually. Children are deeply traumatized by this early sexualization.[7]

Kirsten Jensen with Defend Young Minds makes these proactive suggestions:

- No technology at a young age. A smartphone at grades two, three, and four will result in huge problems. When the phone is introduced (the older the better, grade eight at the earliest) there must be a family plan to teach, supervise and mentor. We must be very careful with technology.
- Know the vulnerability of your child. Know your child. Pay attention to your child.
- Do not give a child a device. Lend yours under specific conditions.
- Know every password.
- Be ahead of the curve and be proactive.
- Find every positive resource available to motivate youth to develop safe patterns.
- Lead by example.
- Take care of your child's emotional needs.
- Develop safe screen habits and manage technology so it helps and does not hurt.
- Be consistent and compassionate and increase awareness. Increase awareness by role-playing, "What would you do if?"

On a global scale, tech companies and the tech sector has been allowed to self-regulate and use voluntary compliance. This has led to a massive volume of misuse. NCOSE, the National Coalition on Sexual Exploitation in the USA, has been particularly active in focusing on policy action regarding online platforms. Traffickers rely on technology to advertise and solicit business.

In late 2022 a timely Canadian Public Safety webinar addressed the impact of technology stating there needs to be:

- Prevention and safety by design.
- Proactive monitoring.
- Content removal and blocking of websites as needed.
- Liability for exploitative content.
- Codes of conduct.
- Identification of exploitative content.

Governments, the private sector, civil society and law enforcement all need to be involved. The concern is that with each year the problems with online exploitation are compounded. Governments lack awareness of the scale of the problem. There is a lack of will or urgency to address the problem, which is currently at an industrial scale (see Valiant Richey in Chapter 27 under Global Initiatives).

The question is, "Who is protecting the children online?"

Answer: Nobody.

Endnotes

1 "Lack of Digital Supervision is Leaving Kids Vulnerable to a Growing Groups of Online Predators: Their Peers" Federation for the Humanities and Social Sciences, May 23, 2021. Charlene Doak-Gebauer is a leading author, international speaker, and founder of the London, Ontario based Internet Sense First charity. She teaches digital supervision in order to protect youth and children online.

2 "Rehtaeh Parsons documentary continues shedding light on story" by Chris Stoodley, Halifax City News, November 22, 2020.
   "Accused in Amanda Todd cyber bullying case alleged to have used 22 accounts to sextort teen" by Jason Proctor, CBC News, June 6, 2022. Amanda Todd became the public face in the fight against cyber bullying after her death by suicide in October 2012. Aydin Coban from the Netherlands was charged for sextortion.

3 Defend Young Minds. This organization helps to prepare kids to reject pornography as part of "digital self-defence." The goal is to raise empowered, resilient, screen-smart kids. defendyoungminds.com

4 Protect Young Eyes. This organization explains digital trends, social media and parental controls and teaches internet safety. protectyoungeyes.com

5 In current news the FBI is warning of an "explosion" in cases of teenagers and young boys being tricked into sending explicit pictures online. BBC News, Washington, December 20, 2022. bbc.com

6 "Extreme internet porn is fuelling a surge in sex attacks by children: Number of under 17s convicted of rape almost doubles in four years" by Ian Drury, Home Affairs Editor, Daily Mail, February 12, 2017.

7 "Mothers Against Sexual Exploitation/Defeating a Predatory Industry" National Centre on Sexual Exploitation. youtube.com

CHAPTER 17

Social Media

"Sexual exploitation of youth
in Canada is worsening."

DR. ROBERT CHRISMAS

Author of "Sex Industry Slavery; Protecting Canada's Youth"

"You learn the hard way.
That's the thing with social media.
Nobody knows what they're doing."

CAMERON DALLAS

According to the Canadian Centre To End Human Trafficking (CCTEHT) National Report 2021, Canadians are not aware of human trafficking, and they do not know the indicators of sexual exploitation and human trafficking. Most luring and grooming for sexual exploitation are now occurring online, primarily on social media sites. The big four social media platforms are Facebook, Instagram, Snapchat and Twitter. TikTok, Discord, Metaverse (which is including VR or virtual reality), and Kik, are other popular platforms. Experts state the "well is poisoned" with these platforms because there is ineffective age verification processes and there is strong indications of underage sexual exploitation. Peer reviewed studies demonstrate significant trauma and damage with overuse.[1]

The spread of child sexual abuse material or child pornography exploded with the rise of the internet, and child sex trafficking is increasing with exposure to a greater market online. Today the problem is complex and still growing. Technology is playing an increasing role in grooming and controlling victims of domestic minor sex trafficking (DMST) and child sex trafficking (CST).

Tiana Sharifi is a sexual exploitation prevention educator and the founder of Sexual Exploitation Education (SEE). She describes how traffickers use social media to lure and groom victims. She examines current trends, different forms of exploitation and the exploiters. She provides a virtual curriculum and is licensed in schools across Canada. She also provides consulting service and has created the first ever anti-sexual exploitation app.

The current online grooming trends involve inviting youth to parties, inviting youth out of town, getting youth to switch platforms, giving expensive gifts, offering modelling gigs and offering quick cash schemes. Youth who go to the parties can be offered drugs and alcohol, then gang raped and filmed. This is a typical scenario for sextortion of the youth. Sextortion is blackmail. According to Cybertip.ca "it is when someone online threatens to send a sexual image or video of you to other people if you don't pay the person or provide more sexual content."

Online the traffickers will establish a connection often through Facebook or dating apps, provide attention to the youth, ensure secrecy, engage in sexual conversation, and then will ask for nude photos or live streaming and a video chat. The videos can be recorded then uploaded to porn sites. To deglamorize the situation, Tiana Sharifi shares real stories with the youth she presents to.

The important message to youth: anything online can be permanent and searchable. She says, "Take a five second time out before clicking send, do not accept any gift of any form online, even live streaming is not private."

Tiana stresses that the notion of "stranger danger" does not work with youth because everyone online is a "friend or follower." She points out that healthy friends and followers do not:

- Ask for personal information.
- Keep conversations private.
- Already know things about you.
- Ask a lot of questions and look to learn more.
- Always agree with you unless you go against what they want.
- Want to see you in a vulnerable state.
- Tell you that your family and friends do not appreciate or understand you.
- Ask for pictures, especially naked or half naked pictures.
- Give gifts.
- Transfer you between platforms.

Healthy boundaries are important to understand online. Youth want to understand what healthy relationships look like and the same principles for boundaries apply in person and online. For example, in person, the other person shows respect for your boundaries, it is not normal for a stranger to compliment you sexually, to offer ways to make you money, will not ask you to flash yourself for money, and a true love interest will not pressure you into sexual activity.

Tiana explains that youth online are self-exploiting themselves by selling their own photos online. These youth have a false sense of security online which sets them up for easier exploitation. Being told about the law does not deter youth from self-exploitation or sexting, but Tiana has found that having conversations with an adult, in a mentorship capacity does deter youth. If adults take the time to educate, speak with and connect with youth, the youth are more likely to listen, consider and change their online activities. Ultimately youth want good lives and want to live well and do not want to be exploited and harmed. Youth need love, desire acceptance, want basic necessities and want to belong, so focusing on healthy versus unhealthy online behaviours is another useful strategy for educating and protecting them.

Children of the Street advocates for online safety planning in preparation for online encounters. They have a downloadable PDF called Have the Talk on childrenofthestreet.com. Safety strategies are:
• Block.
• Delete.
• Report (Kids Help Phone).
• If feeling unsafe, stop talking to them, don't do what they're asking, screenshot their messages and share the messages with a safe adult.

In the USA, the successful prevention education organization called Protect Young Eyes shares top tactics they teach to keep youth safe online:
• Right tech at the right time.
• No social media or smartphones until age fifteen years plus.
• All digital devices are co-owned.
• Caring control. Not just parental control.
• Shoulder-to-shoulder screen time. (Do this together; team approach).
• Scaffolding (trust building).

"Parenting in the Digital Age" is a topic this organization prioritizes. Since 2015, this group has helped to create an internet-ready home; a home that is free from porn, predators and problems. They take complex digital topics and make them understandable. They present regularly at global conferences on sexual exploitation.

Dr. Jean Twenge,[2] professor from San Diego and media researcher wrote the new book called *iGen, Why Today's Super-Connected Kids Are Growing Up Less Rebellious, More Tolerant, Less Happy and Completely Unprepared for Adulthood.* Her book describes Gen Z (1997–2012) who are "growing up on digital technology" with over 50% owning smartphones. In her research Dr. Twenge discovered a sudden change in this demographic. They are more likely to be depressed and anxious, have suicide risk factors and are twice as likely to be unhappy compared to any other age group. Her recommendation for Generation Z: "Use the phone for good things, one to two hours a day, then go for a run, swim, visit a friend in person, and live life. Let the smart phone be a tool, not a tool that uses you."

Jesse Miller[3] from the University of Victoria, B.C. is another educator with expertise in social media who believes that media education for youth today is critical. He claims that digital citizenship applies to all of us, and that social media has a big role in our lives. His focus is on teaching the importance of healthy participation online and media literacy.

Jesse emphasizes that violating privacy is not acceptable. His goal is to empower youth, so they have open communications and safe sharing online. Our culture is multi-connected, and it is imperative to be responsible with these tools. Jesse suggests that social media gives us a version of events, but does not give us the complete picture.

The question he says we need to ask is, "Are we generating ethical, reflective, media literate users of mobile communication tools and social sharing platforms?" It is imperative to have good empathy and ethics in the social media space and to teach our children critical thinking skills.

Jesse asks these questions regarding digital consent:
- Did you ask for permission to share an image or picture?
- Are you sharing information without informing the person it may impact?
- Are you taking a screenshot for selfish purposes?
- Are you leveraging information over another? This may be illegal.
- Illegal content on your device may impact you in a variety of ways.
- Share with care.

Tania Haigh is the Founder of Kids Too Movement[4] and Parents Against Child Abuse.[5] She states that while some social media sites are providing tools for parents to have access to their children's activities online, the onus is on parents. Social media platforms will typically have the bare minimum for controls to protect the youngest users. There needs to be legislation and regulation (the USA has the Earn It Act) to hold social media platforms accountable for allowing child pornography to circulate and to stop them from protecting predators while prioritizing profit over the hearts and minds of our children.

Technology is quickly advancing on our youth. How can they stay safe online when there is so much content constantly coming at them? It can be very discouraging. Youth are being bombarded with messages that undermine their worth and leave them feeling empty, hopeless and vulnerable. Youth need to be empowered to make healthy media choices. Media literacy is important. Critical thinking is key so that girls aren't at risk of being sexualized and boys do not become desensitized. Peer to peer programs run by student leaders are effective and can help to facilitate important discussions. The trends in social media are concerning and changing very quickly. The COVID-19 pandemic accelerated the dangers online because youth were spending much more time online.

One platform that is particularly exploitative is OnlyFans that originated in the UK. While it is portrayed as a mainstream platform, it is an online adult website. Traffickers will encourage young people to join it to make money. The appeal to make huge amounts of money in a short time has created the problem of serious exploitation through slow grooming. Money, power and control draw exploiters to this platform. The recruiting is aggressive because the recruiters are paid. It is trendy and modern but has a fake veneer with layers of exploitation. It is an open door for human traffickers because it is a difficult platform to monitor and search by police. Other platforms are following suit.

Harmony Grillo[6] is a survivor who produced a timely video called, "What No One's Telling You About OnlyFans" and gives ten reasons for youth to stay off. She summarizes these points:

- There is leaked content, piracy and the content is bought and sold.
- A participant will always be asked to do more. There is a black hole of demand.
- The money is not what they tell you. Exploiters will ask for more novelty and sexualization. Dehumanization begins at this point.
- There is a huge cost to becoming a sexual object. Becoming a product is a job requirement.
- Sexual harassment occurs because the participant is expected to interact with subscribers. This is sexual abuse.
- Stalkers are there.
- It will interfere with personal goals and your future because someone will see it.
- It will change you. Participants lose themselves to someone else's fantasy. You are no longer a real authentic person.
- Reduces ability to have healthy and real relationships. Once photos are out there, you cannot take them back.

- If the money is good, the cost is very high, and participants are left with trauma. The money is not worth it. The degradation is not worth it.
- Harmony ends with, "You are valuable, and you are here for a reason. You are worth far more."

The National Center on Sexual Exploitation (NCOSE)[7] sponsors a Stand Week: Media Safety for Youth designed for eleven to fourteen-year-olds:

- STAND UP to look up and be present, prioritizing real relationships over screens.
- STAND OUT by being true to myself in person and online.
- STAND WITH those who are alone, excluded or vulnerable.
- STAND FOR positive media, valuing the dignity of others and myself.
- STAND NOW and be a leader of positive technology.

Endnotes

1. Online Child Sexual Exploitation. From Public Safety Canada. As technology has advanced, child sexual exploitation has drastically increased in Canada. Cybertip.ca has processed millions of child sexual exploitation reports. canada.ca
2. "iGen, why today's super-connected kids are growing up less rebellious, more tolerant, less happy and completely unprepared for adulthood" by Dr. Jean Twenge, published by Atria Books, August 22, 2017.
3. Jesse Miller is trainer with Safer Schools Together: Digital Threat Assessment Training saferschoolstogether.com
4. KIDS TOO addresses child protection for the modern day parent. kidstoo.org
5. P.A.X.A. Parents Against Child Sex Abuse. This is a non-profit dedicated to empowering parents to protect their children from sexual abuse. paxa.online
6. Harmony Grillo. Harmony has written books, started an NGO and is a prolific speaker on the issue of sexual exploitation. harmonygrillo.com
7. NCOSE, National Center on Sexual Exploitation, in Washington, DC. This organization strategizes to combat sexual abuse and exploitation with a multi-faceted and interdisciplinary approach. In particular they expose the connections and roots of the systems, which support and sustain sexual abuse and exploitation. They mobilize legal, corporate, and legislative action to build a world free from sexual abuse and exploitation with the goal of defending human dignity. endsexualexploitation.org

CHAPTER 18

Cultural Norms, Marketing, Ads

"Learn to say 'No' without explaining yourself."

UNKNOWN

The sexualization of girls and women is overwhelming in media, marketing and our culture and it is important to be aware of the tactics.[1]

Who are the cultural icons? Who do youth and children want to be like and look like? With the bombardment of media, culture is becoming dehumanized. The bombardment of messaging today is to be sexual. Who will have the courage to say "No" to this hyper-sexualization?

Advertisers are targeting and reaching children at younger and younger ages. There is an explosion of children's advertising. Women's bodies are the currency. Male entitlement to power has become normalized and glamorized. Power, intimidation and force are the new masculinity for boys to emulate. Passivity is the female model. How will this effect real life behaviour of men and women? It is difficult to stay healthy in such a toxic cultural environment.

Ads sell through images. They sell values and identify what success looks like. Women see images of female beauty, ideal images based on the flawless imaginings accomplished with cosmetics and computer rendering. Women's bodies are shown as things and objects, which affects a woman's self-esteem.

Turning a human being into an object is the first step to justify violence against that person. Dehumanization allows for violence. Violence and abuse are logical results of objectification. Girls tend to feel fine about themselves when they are eight to ten years old, then at adolescence they frequently hit a wall. They become lost, confused, self-doubting and vulnerable. Girls are being groomed by this toxic culture, which alters their values and beliefs into accepting their own victimization and exploitation.

Having ongoing conversations with youth and children about these trends is important. As Jesse Miller pointed out in the last chapter, we need to teach critical thinking skills to our youth.

Endnotes

1   Report of the APA Task Force on the Sexualization of Girls, American Psychological Association, 2007. apa.org/pi/women/programs/girls

CHAPTER 19

Pornography

> "I want to talk about the internet, the impact it is having on the innocence of our children, how online pornography is corroding childhood and how, in the darkest corners of the internet, there are things going on that are a direct danger to our children, and that must be stamped out."

UK PRIME MINISTER DAVID CAMERON

Speech: The internet and pornography: Prime Minister calls for action, July 22, 2013.

Pornography is the fuel for prostitution, human trafficking, domestic violence, and harm towards women and girls. In fact, pornography is filmed prostitution and a predatory industry.

The porn industry is massive, lucrative, available in unlimited quantities and unchecked globally. A helpful TED Talk by researcher and educator Gary Wilson, aimed at understanding the research on the impact of pornography on the brain, is "The Great Porn Experiment."[1] Key points stood out to me:

- By age ten years boys look for porn.
- By age twelve years 90% of boys have watched porn.
- Porn produces impotence and erectile dysfunction.
- Porn viewing is very serious in youngsters because it causes deep 'ruts' in their young developing brains. Ruts are not easily removed.
- The key to the addictive nature of porn is the unending novelty. Porn produces a steady harem, experiencing what most men would never experience in many lifetimes.
- There is a movement for men to unhook from porn.

Another worthwhile TED Talk by educator Ran Gavrieli is "Why I Stopped Porn."[2] Four points stood out to me:
- Porn embodies sexual exploitation.
- A prostitute experiences social death; drugs, STIs, murder, or suicide is the standard result.
- Porn increases the demand for paid sex, so the supply must increase.
- Men should not want to be a part of the sex industry.

Dr. John Foubert[3] is an expert on how pornography harms. His book is *Protecting Your Children from Internet Pornography* by Northfield Publishers. Regarding the prevalence of porn use he states that: half of eighth graders have viewed pornography, typically the first time for boys to see porn is age thirteen, and girls at seventeen. And these ages are dropping quickly. 94% of men have viewed porn in their lifetime, 87% of women. Porn viewing increased during COVID-19. His concern is that violence in pornography is mainstream, and that pornography teaches violence, making it a recipe for rape. Pornography demeans and objectifies women. His research has shown that men will be more likely to rape, commit violence and use sexual force in their own relations, which leads to violence against women.

Dr. Gail Dines[4] is a professor of sociology and women's studies and considered one of the leading anti-porn scholars and activists in the world. She has been researching the porn industry for over thirty years and has written the book *Pornland: How Porn has Hijacked Our Sexuality.* Her TED Talk "Growing up in a Pornified Culture" gives a concise comment on the danger and harm porn is to a healthy culture. The harm is real and measurable. Porn is so omnipresent in today's culture that it is a public health concern we cannot ignore. Porn online is unregulated. Tobacco and alcohol are regulated, so why does porn get a pass? Porn is the public health crisis of the digital age.

Dr. Dines visited and presented in Vancouver. During her presentations session she described her goal to produce "Healthy Sex Curriculum." Her organization, Culture Reframed, is a program for parents, educators and medical practitioners. She gives an overview on "What is porn?" and "How do I talk about it"?

For example, sample topics for parents of tweens:
- Boundaries, consent, privacy.
- Managing technology.
- Navigating online and offline relationships.
- Leading discussions skilfully.

Sample topics for parents of teens:
- Physical and emotional and cognitive development of teens.
- Healthy relationships.
- Toxic unhealthy masculinity.
- Sexting and digital footprint.
- Predators, human trafficking, safety.

Pornography, prostitution and trafficking are all inter-related. Many women in porn are trafficked. Dr. Dines supports the Nordic Model or "Equality Model" that we currently have with Canada's PCEPA Law.

The question she asks her students is, "What do you, as women and men want in your lives?" The answer she receives from them is that they want a life of dignity and respect.

Dr. Dines' focus on sex and porn in the digital age and what to do about it is described on her Cultureframed.org website. Her point is that online porn engenders violence against women. Young people are growing up in a digital society that is image based and there is no escaping its influence. In contrast, as parents, most of us grew up with the printed word. Now, porn is the major source of sex education in the world by default because of easy access to it online. Parents, pediatricians and educators should be first in line to protect children. But pornographers have effectively hijacked the education about our sexuality.

The boundaries of our private lives are stressed, and culturally there is a dramatic shift to where everyone wants to be documented. In thirty years, Dr. Dines has seen a dramatic change in her students. Our sexualized culture is doing the work of grooming women for the benefit of the abuser.

The availability of pornography exploded with the advent of the internet. One third of internet watched content is pornography; more than Netflix, Amazon and Twitter combined. It has become a massive, lucrative industry. She states that Mindgeek-Pornhub, has become the "Walmart of Porn" with the target viewer an eleven-year-old boy.

Porn offers novelty, risk taking and sexual identity. Ninety percent of porn contains violence against women. For a young boy viewing porn, it becomes his initiation into masculinity, and he sees violent sexuality as normal. Porn lays a trap or web for the young boy, and he is catapulted into a world of abuse. He becomes ashamed, self-loathing but aroused, producing deep trauma in his psyche. If this is not resolved, the trauma gets deeper. Pornography has produced a generation of boys with PTSD, with addiction the result. Porn releases more dopamine than drugs. Boys have been targeted aggressively, and the girls are next. This is the business plan of the porn industry.

Dr. Dines has studied the effects of porn for forty years and she notes that it limits intimacy and connectedness. It increases risky behaviours, anxiety and depression. While the situation is troubling, Dr. Dines encourages the public to "tie the monster down piece by piece." The two protective areas to address porn are good parental supports and quality healthcare.

As a culture we must produce porn-resistant children. One exposure to pornography can change the way a child thinks. Mindful parenting is key. As parents we need to help our children develop positive peer relationships and teach our boys empathy and encourage them to have their own personal moral compass and build up their core values. What do they want to be? Who do they want to become? Explain that sex and love are not the same. Explain that sex is natural, normal and beautiful but porn hijacks sexuality, mental health and healthy sexual development. Porn promotes rape culture.

Dr. Dines encourages parents to start class action suits against the porn producers, and to make as much noise as possible including going to schools to ask if porn is being addressed. She believes that exploiters need to be held accountable to reset social norms and help survivors find justice.

Central to porn is profit making. Women are hurt by porn. Somehow the profit motive needs to be removed. To reiterate, pediatricians and educators along with parents need to be frontline in battling porn use.

Dr. Dines travels the world and presents to global conferences. She believes addressing porn is a critical human rights and justice issue and one that every government should be committed to if they are committed to girls and women's equality. Thousands of girls have disclosed to her the role of porn in their abuse.

Porn subtly undermines the collective wellbeing of men. Porn destroys the three skills that sustain society: the ability for intimacy, connection and empathy. Girls and women are at risk when they become sex objects because this normalizes sexual harassment, legitimizes sex acts that debase and degrade women and it grooms young girls to be objectified.

Porn is not benign. It is a multi-billion dollar industry that is reshaping our world. Porn has become the major form of sex education in the world and is sold as a commercial product. The message it expresses is that women exist for sexual use and abuse. Dr. Dines concludes that we have a macro-social problem. It is a gendered issue about oppression, inequality and male dominance. The question is what is going to happen to this generation of boys and girls who have grown-up on hard-core pornography? Ultimately men are the ones who will decide to make this world a decent place and a better place for women and children.

A recent investigative report on pornography was the W5 program by top Canadian journalist Victor Malarek called Generation XXX on "Freely available online pornography exposes children to violent, abusive sex." He interviews twelve-year-old Joseph Deschambault who became a porn addict on his family's computer at age nine.[5]

The one thing all porn addicts have in common is no parental discussions about sex. And Dr. Dines adds, "We must talk to our children about pornography otherwise pornography talks to our children."

Endnotes

1 "The Great Porn Experiment" by Gary Wilson, TEDx Glasgow, May 16, 2012.
2 "Why I Stopped Porn" by Ran Gavrieli, TEDx Jaffa, August 2016.
3 "Dr. John Foubert speaks out on porn's connections to sexual violence/truth about porn" Dr. John Foubert is an interdisciplinary scholar with over 50 peer-reviewed publications that have appeared in some of the top-ranked journals in Education, Psychology, and Gender Studies. fightthenewdrug.org
4 "Pornland: How Porn Has Hijacked Our Sexuality" by Dr. Gail Dines, 2010 Beacon Press, Boston. Dr. Dines is an anti-porn scholar, activist and speaker. She is founder and president of the non-profit organization Culture Reframed that is dedicated to building resilience and resistance in youth to hyper-sexualized media and porn. She researches from a public health perspective. gaildines.com
5 Victor Malarek program on W5 addressing youth porn use. ctvnews.ca

CHAPTER 20

Experts on Porn

"There is no dignity
when the human dimension is
eliminated from the person.
In short, the problem with pornography
is not it shows too much of the person,
but that it shows far too little."

POPE JOHN PAUL II

One of the best resources in the country for the prevention of online sexual exploitation is the Canadian Centre of Protection of Children C3P (Chapter 14). [1] The C3P is a national charity educating the public on ways to keep Canadian children safe. The C3P operates Canada's National Tip Line (1-866-658-9022) to address online sexual exploitation. It is part of a national strategy to protect children online. Lianna McDonald is the executive director. Her observation is the number of reports of cyber bullying per month are dramatically increasing, representing a growing proliferation of child sexual abuse on the internet. Internet use has accelerated and is normalizing the sexualization of children, making it easier for offenders to participate in this illegal behaviour. Incidences of child porn remain online and can propagate indefinitely. Parents have nowhere to report in Canada, so they call the Tip Line.

Pornography content has become increasingly disturbing over the years and includes sadism, bondage, torture and bestiality. The public is reporting that it is in plain view on popular social media platforms.

The internet has become a tool for sexual offenders to groom children. Sexual offenders show children these sites to lower children's inhibitions. Porn is used to educate the child on what the offender wants the child to do.

Adolescents have easy access to pornographic material contributing to depression, violence and sexual deviancy. In 2016 C3P found that 70% of students in grades six had come across online porn. Eleven to sixteen-year-olds were shocked and confused initially then this subsided as half of the boys saw porn as realistic and a source of ideas of what they would try out. In a survey with parents, C3P found that parents were deeply concerned and wanted help to educate and protect their children.

In 2017, a number of experts testified to the Federal Health Committee about the impacts of porn on our culture and our children. Three experts stood out to me: Dr. Sharon Cooper, Ms. Cordelia Anderson and Dr. Mary Anne Layden.

Dr. Sharon Cooper[2] is a forensic pediatrician working and researching in the area of child maltreatment for forty years. She sees internet porn as a significant threat to children today. She concludes that everyone is affected by porn; the child, family, community, and society. Porn is used to indoctrinate and seduce children. Adults use porn to entice children and as black mail in sextortion. Children become disinhibited and then assault younger children, creating a downward spiral where porn becomes a visual invitation for more egregious behaviour. From a public health perspective, porn is more than an image being viewed; people experience what they view. Cooper states, "What you see is what you get but it is actually what you see is what gets you. It is a slippery slope when sexual harm becomes normal."

Ms. Cordelia Anderson[3] is founder of Sensibilities Prevention Services who started one of the first child sexual abuse prevention programs in the United States. She makes the point that the brain is very malleable, responds to novelty and is wired for reward. Culture is widely impacted, because even if a child is blocked from porn they are still influenced by the expectation of other children. A disturbing trend is child-on-child sexual assault as a result of porn viewing. There are no studies that show porn is helpful or healthful for children, youth or culture, yet there are myriad studies showing the polluting effect on health and wellness. The porn industry needs to be held accountable for the harm caused. Parents must monitor and filter the internet for their children otherwise it is not safe.

Bike helmets, child car seats, seat belts and tobacco use have all been areas of concern for public health, with successful campaigns to mitigate harm. Pornography will need a similar coordinated public health approach to warn of its harms and addictive qualities. There needs to be broad based policies to limit porn use. The brain is not mature until age twenty-five and therefore is particularly vulnerable to harm. There needs to be a counter-narrative to porn use because it harms individuals and families. Open ongoing conversation with your children and your family is the best tool.

Dr. Mary Anne Layden,[4] a sexual trauma expert states that society is now "pornified." The result is that the body is seen as a commodity. Sex is perceived as a product that can be bought and sold. Pornography, prostitution and trafficking are interconnected. Pornography teaches that sexual violence is normal and doesn't hurt anyone. Porn is not about intimacy, caring, love or respect. Porn is not about marriage or family.

Porn sex is recreational, and you do not need to know your partner; it is a one-way street. Performers in porn films never say no.

Dr. Layden's research findings are concerning: many men who watch porn think women enjoy being raped; accepting the violence. Increasingly men see women as sex objects and become less satisfied with their partners. Increased porn viewing is related to higher psychopathic scores. In younger men especially there is erectile dysfunction. There is less brain connectivity. These men are more likely to sexually abuse, harass, rape, and coerce sex with drugs and alcohol. The younger the boys are when watching porn, the more likely they are to participate in non-consenting sex. The research shows that children who are exposed to sexual media are more likely to engage in what they view. There is a greater use of porn among sex offenders, child offenders and incest offenders. Many men who watch child porn admit abusing children as well.

There are three main factors connected with sexual violence:
- Hostility toward women.
- Sex is casual and violent.
- The use of porn.

Dr. Layden summarizes, "The main damage of porn is it threatens the loss of love, in a world where only love can bring happiness."

There are numerous experts who study the impact of porn on the brain. Dr. Gary Wilson's book *Your Brain on Porn*[5] studies the neuroscience and addiction to violent porn. He states that boys and men get off on the violence and the power, rather than sex itself.

There is a recovery industry to help viewers stop porn, such as "Fight the New Drug"[6] by Clayton Olsen who started the "Fortify" program. Fight the New Drug has compiled short video vignettes with the experts speaking on the harmful effects of pornography. These are found at Truthaboutporn.org, a current and ever-growing database to collect research. For example, Heidi Olsen[7] a Sexual Assault Nurse Examiner at a large children's hospital summarizes the concerning trends with youth. Since 2015, she has seen eleven to fifteen-year-olds that were the sexual perpetrators. Olsen and her team are seeing more youth act out in very violent harmful ways and are finding that these boys are victims of watching pornography. Her conclusion: there is a direct correlation with watching porn and acting out sexually.

The pornography industry is all about money. Porn-viewing starting age is typically eleven to twelve years and getting younger. According to Holly-ann Martin with Safe4Kids[8] in Australia, children as young as four and five are reported viewing porn. They may act out on what they view. She reports that children as young as four will take pictures of themselves. Five-year-olds will type in XXX or ask Siri for porn. Holly-ann Martin states parents must protect their children by:

- Being engaged.
- Setting limits on social media use.
- Do not assume youth/children are not viewing.
- Inform them of the risks and dangers of the internet and social media.
- Have open dialogue.
- Know where to turn for help.

Dr. Jocelyn Monsma Selby asked me to present at the inaugural global summit on the impact of porn on youth, "Stronger Together-Protecting Children from Online Pornography by Inviting a Public Health Response."[9] Global researchers and academics including Dr. Gail Dines and Dr. John Foubert made compelling presentations. The influence of pornography on our culture is shocking and pervasive because it is expressed as the six As:

- Accessible.
- Anonymous.
- Affordable.
- Acceptable.
- Aggressive.
- Addictive.

Liz Walker, from Brisbane, Australia[10] was an organizer for this global summit and has a master's degree in health sciences and sexual health. She summarizes the impacts of children accessing pornography:
- Linked to body insecurity, depression, and mental health issues.
- Triggers compulsion, sexual dysfunction, and arousal disorder.
- Shapes arousal pathways including illegal acts such as incest and paedophilia.
- Is a grooming tool and normalizes harmful behaviours and exploitation.
- Provokes self-exploitation, sexting, and revenge porn.
- Promotes high-risk acts.
- Demonstrates child-on-child and peer-on-peer sexual abuse.
- Reinforces sexism, racism, and objectification.
- Fuels child sexual exploitation/sex trafficking.
- Eroticizes sexual aggression and violence.
- Parents using porn can contribute unsafe environments and family breakdowns.
- Early exposure can cause trauma and develop mental issues.

Pornography is a public health crisis. Along with childhood sexual assault, pornography is a pipeline to prostitution. Once prostitution is normalized, then demand for it will increase. Trafficking and child sex trafficking in turn will increase to satisfy the growing demand. A public health approach is needed to hold accountable the porn industry and tech companies that facilitate sexual exploitation.

Endnotes

1   Canadian Centre for Protection of Children. protectchildren.ca
2   Dr. Sharon Cooper MD is CEO of Developmental and Forensic Pediatrics, a consulting firm which provides medical care, research, training and expert witness experience in child maltreatment cases. connectsafely.org/sharon-cooper/
    "Sharon Cooper: Because of the internet, kids can be trafficked in a lot of ways" youtube.com
3   "A Public Health Approach to Pornography" by Ms. Cordelia Anderson, April 17, 2017. vimeo.com
4   "Dr. Mary Anne Layden, Ph.D. Interview // Truth About Porn" November 4, 2016. Dr. Mary Anne Layden Ph.D. is a psychotherapist and Director of Education at the Center for Cognitive Therapy at the University of Pennsylvania. She is the Director of the Sexual Trauma and Psychopathology Program and the Director of the Social Action Committee for Women's Psychological Health. Dr. Layden is a leading expert on pornography addiction. fightthenewdrug.org
5   Gary Wilson. yourbrainonporn.com
6   There are many articles available to view. fightthenewdrug.org
7   Video by SANE nurse Heidi Olson on "The Truth About Porn" video series sponsored by Fight the New Drug: fightthenewdrug.org/heidi-olson-sane-nurse-assault-video/
8   Safe4Kids is a company based in Perth, Western Australia that specializes in child protection education, which is also known as child abuse prevention education, protective behaviours and body safety. They train parents, teachers and educators in Australia and internationally. safe4kids.com.au
9   "Connecting to Protect: Connecting to Protect Children in the Digital Age" This is a world-first global initiative to tackle children and young people's online pornography access focusing on mental health and safety consequences. connectingtoprotect.org
10 Liz Walker is an educator and advocate responding to porn harms. She was a co-director for the Connecting to Protect conference in Canada, University of Calgary, Department of Social Work.lizwalkerpresents.com

CHAPTER 21

Prevention

"Although the world is full of suffering, it is also full of the overcoming of it."

HELEN KELLER

Awareness is prevention. To create systemic change in society there needs to be awareness, prevention education, active collaboration, intervention and a reduction of demand for paid sex. Human trafficking is a global crime and countries around the world are realizing that it must be stopped.[1]

How can human trafficking be prevented? Clearly, the federal government has the power to put laws into place that identify the crime and set action plans in motion to accomplish this. Former member of parliament Joy Smith successfully introduced two private members bills that became the first laws in Canada to address human trafficking. Another law was then necessary to tackle the root causes of prostitution specifically. The federal law, the Protection of Communities and Exploited Persons Act (PCEPA), does that. PCEPA makes it illegal to purchase sex in Canada while decriminalizing its sale to protect those who are exploited by others.

Since 2015, for the first time in Canada, we have a law that criminalizes the root cause of harm, the sex buyer. If PCEPA is repealed, then sex buyers will be able to buy sex undeterred. Valiant Richey, the special advisor on human trafficking for the OSCE warns of this outcome (Chapter 27). He is unequivocal in his statements that human trafficking is currently an out-of-control problem globally, and unless the demand for commercially paid sex is discouraged, the plague of human trafficking will continue.

The effectiveness of PCEPA depends on consistent enforcement, which requires buy-in from law enforcement. In turn, crown counsel and prosecutors need to buy-in and be willing to bring forward charges and sentencing.

The purpose of the Canadian PCEPA law is to target the root cause of harm, the sex buyer. A research-based, experience-driven resource is DemandForum.org by Dr. Michael Shively,[2] who studies the demand side of prostitution. The sex buyer tends to be invisible when prostitution is discussed. Who are the sex buyers? What will stop sex buyers from buying? After all, if there are no sex buyers, there will be no sex industry. Dr. Shively has studied the results on recidivism rates of participants in John Schools where charged sex buyers are educated about the harm of prostitution and the harm they have caused to women and girls when buying sex. Dr. Shively has observed American cities that have implemented John Schools report that there is a 40% to 70 % reduction in the market activity without changing laws. He concludes that John Schools work. He also found that sex buyers are not criminals; they are ordinary people that need an incentive to stop buying sex. The threat of being arrested is what works.

Valiant Richey and Dr. Michael Shively recognize the importance of online education and the necessity of reaching men and boys before they buy sex. As a society and culture, we need to make sex buying undesirable and to be seen as a negative and harmful activity.

> "The first step in understanding the sex industry is to understand the customers, the johns."

JOSEPH PARKER

Sex buyers want younger and younger women, including youth and children. The Canadian Centre for Child Protection[3] is dedicated to personal safety of all children. To prevent sexual exploitation, they recommend to families:

- Be aware.
- Establish rules in the home.
- Know settings and set up privacy settings on computers and devices.
- Supervise.
- Have unplug times such as during meals and overnight.
- Stay informed. Sign up for cyber tip alerts.
- Have regular age-appropriate conversations with youth.
- Warn about live streaming because it can be recorded.
- Help children set up privacy settings.
- Remove devices before bed.
- Reassure youth you are there to help them.
- Check in with children regularly. Ask direct questions. "Have you seen anything weird, uncomfortable or inappropriate online?"
- Practice responding by role-playing.
- Stay curious and listen.
- Check out resources, for example protectkidsonline.ca

Cybertip.ca provides public education and resources, support and referral services to help Canadians keep their families safe. They receive reports from the public regarding:

- Child sexual abuse material.
- Online luring.
- Commercial sexual exploitation of children.
- Travelling to sexually exploit a child.
- Trafficking of children.
- Making sexually explicit material available to a child.
- Agreement or arrangement with another person to commit a sexual offence against a child.

> "A child has a greater chance of being sexually abused than burned in a fire. Along with stop, drop, and roll we must teach them to yell, run, and tell."
>
> CAROLYN BYERS RUCH

An effective organization is Thorn.org in the USA founded by actors Ashton Kutcher and Demi Moore. They have a bold goal: to eliminate child sexual abuse from the internet. They use advanced technology to help build a safer internet and to defend children from sexual abuse. The Thorn website is excellent and full of research, statistics and solutions.

Another effective prevention program trainer is Tania Haigh with the "Kids, Too" program. Kidstoo.org is a follow up to the #MeToo campaign. Tania set it up to empower parents by focusing on how to stay safe online and at school. She says it is very important to get a handle on a school's online and tech usage policies. At school it is important to know who your child's friends and contacts are. Teach children the difference between online friends versus real-time friends. Explain that online friends can turn into offline meetings of predators.

Tania stresses that parents need to be involved and to ask questions so that children are protected. Tania is positive in her presentations and encourages parents and families to protect their youth. The most common scenario is that parents do not believe anything can happen to their children. To prepare children, it is important to teach them about sexual abuse and the trend of child-on-child sexual abuse. There can be student or adult predators at any school.

> "Don't put your child at risk.
> Limit unsupervised one-on-one time between your
> child and another adult or another child."
>
> CAROLYN BYERS RUCH

Police officer Dominic Monchamp from the Montreal vice unit has seen the results of human trafficking in schools. He sees girls deceived by boyfriends at school, in malls or on Facebook and then the reality of finding them suffering the effects of PTSD and Stockholm Syndrome at the hands of traffickers. Traffickers are "cool" guys at first, targeting girls by looking for their vulnerabilities. He states that to aggressively prevent predation there needs to be strong police partnerships with parents, schools, youth and health centres and education about this crime. Officer Monchamp provides an excellent online slide show presentation that is worth viewing.[4]

The good news is there is some repercussion developing from the public with the recognition that boys and girls are being robbed of their beauty and potential. We can all make a difference to expose and stop this crime.

"I was just four when a hired teenage fieldhand attempted to molest me. Miraculously, I got away, and I told my dad. My father made three important choices that day: He listened to me, he believed me, and he took action. I was one of the fortunate ones—I had a childhood."

CAROLYN BYERS RUCH

Endnotes

1   "Preventing sexual exploitation of children and youth" British Columbia Public Safety. www2.gov.bc.ca
"Stopping the Sexual Exploitation of Children and Youth" British Columbia Ministry of Public Safety and Solicitor General, Victim Services and Crime Prevention. This is a 20-page booklet with tools and resources.
"Preventing the Sexual Exploitation of Children and Youth in the Lower Mainland" Pacific Community resources Society (PCRS). This is a toolkit created by the Stop Exploiting Youth (SEY) team in response to the Stop the Sexual Exploitation of Children and Youth Awareness Week occurring March 8, 2021 to March 14, 2021. empowersurrey.ca
"Child Sexual Exploitation on the Internet" Public Safety Canada. publicsafety.gc.ca
2   Dr. Michael Shively, Ph.D., Senior Advisor on Research and Policy, National Centre on Sexual Exploitation. demand-forum.org
3   Canada's National tipline for reporting the online sexual exploitation of children. cybertip.ca
4   Dominic Monchamp presentation on human trafficking. traffickinginpersonssymposium.files.wordpress.com/2012/03/presentation-of-the-montrc3a9al-police-service-english-1.pdf

CHAPTER 22

Law Enforcement Agencies

"To Protect and to Serve."

POLICE MOTTO

Safe, secure communities are needed today more than ever because of increased and undeterred criminal activity—including the drug epidemic, gang crime and recruitment, and the increase in sexual assault and child exploitation. Law enforcement and community policing is key to uphold law and order to maintain safe civil communities. Compassionate, trauma-informed, well-trained police who are well supported and well-funded are needed.

The main challenge for law enforcement is that the crime of human trafficking is highly lucrative and growing fast. Trafficked individuals are seen as the most profitable commodity because they can be used and then sold again and again. Little or no start-up money is required, and there are few consequences of getting caught. However, when the public and police become educated about the crime and work collaboratively, the dial can be turned back on this crime.

Law and law enforcement are not enough to change the culture or stop the crime, but laws give the framework for what society values and considers important. The laws must be maintained and supported by society to work. Law enforcement is crucial in stopping human trafficking. Without effective law enforcement criminals will be emboldened and crime will increase.

With human trafficking the process of addressing the crime needs to be streamlined with a prescribed procedure for police. Police agencies must collaborate because human trafficking is a difficult, fluid, always changing crime. Delay is an impediment and officers typically need to move quickly. The ability of police to detect human trafficking varies by resources, training, and specialized units available. The more resources and training the better to categorize the type of trafficking occurring, interview and assist victims and lay charges.

Nunzio Tramontozzi, an officer formerly with the Toronto Police Department, spoke in the Covenant House video called *Amy's Story* [1] which describes the growing problem of human trafficking in Toronto and the GTA. He cites that education is the best tool to keep youth out of the sex industry. He encourages the public to know the indicators of human trafficking and to report to the police.

Tramontozzi describes the traffickers as young men seeking money and power. Toronto is a sex tourism hotspot; proliferating in hotels where trafficking is widespread. He sees girls being run across Canada with their trafficker boyfriends. Girls fall in love with their predator, ending up servicing fifteen to twenty men per day and can make the trafficker hundreds of thousands of dollars per year. Nunzio sees a huge need for the reciprocity of Victim Services across the provinces and the importance of sharing information.

Joy Smith works closely with law enforcement and her son is an RCMP officer in Manitoba. I learned from Joy that collaborating closely with law enforcement is imperative if the crime of human trafficking is ever going to be stopped.

First meetings with local law enforcement agencies began early in my advocacy work, beginning with the West Vancouver Police Department then the Vancouver Police Department; relationships that have continued ever since. Meetings at B.C. RCMP headquarters have been a particular highlight over the years. Officers in the detachments I have met want training sessions on human trafficking. For example: in the spring of 2022, the RCMP held their first human trafficking webinar series for law enforcement across Canada. It was an honour to present in a series that was well-received.

Because of their work addressing human sex trafficking, my appreciation for law enforcement has increased each year. The challenges faced by law enforcement on a routine basis is often life threatening or extremely disturbing. For example, the Robert Pickton case is the most alarming tragedy involving trafficked and prostituted victims. For anyone to understand this crime, learning about the Pickton case is essential as it exemplifies the brutality of the sex industry. One of the reasons that it took so long for Pickton to be charged is that the law enforcement agencies did not collaborate but operated separately with a silo mentality. Agency collaboration between cities and RCMP will make a difference in solving crimes faster.

As a creative innovation in Manitoba, social workers have been trained and equipped to recognize the indicators of human trafficking. They can enter homes without a warrant, unlike police. Social workers can make charges without a victim having to testify. Vancouver Police Department is now working with embedded social workers, and this is helping to identify trafficked and vulnerable youth.

Former forensic behavioural specialist Dr. Matt Logan[2] is well known in policing circles and became a specialist in dealing with sex offenders. Logan succeeded in getting hardened sexual offenders to confess their crimes by carefronting as a strategy to win over individuals and bring these people to their senses. He learned the value of being a good listener by being empathetic, caring, calm, intuitive and willing to learn from experience. He built bridges out of barricades and gained the trust of the offenders. They became willing to talk about and admit their crimes.

Dr. Logan presented to officers and service providers at an RCMP sponsored training event about the importance of protecting children. From him, we learned that early adolescence, ages eleven to fourteen tend to be the forgotten years, yet these are the ages targeted by the sex industry. Logan's concern is that society is making children into adults too soon and children must be protected during the early adolescence phase. His admonition is that we must show, as families and communities, that we value our children.

He went on to explain that pimps and traffickers have highly developed techniques to groom children and in tandem, the pornography industry is exacerbating the process. The normalizing of pornography with its effects on the adolescent brain is a big problem, evidenced by links between sexual assault and pornography viewing. Pedophiles are a growing danger in society as they groom children. He states that pedophiles also groom the parents so that they have access to their children.

Dr. Logan maintains that early intervention is the answer to prevent criminal and psychopathic behaviour resulting in child predation. He suggests early intervention by twelve years of age or younger. Parents and teachers can identify potential psychopathic behaviour in youth. Between ages twelve to eighteen, 46% of children can potentially swing into an anti-social lifestyle by being influenced by just 6% of deviant individuals.

What causes deviation socially? Childhood rejection especially parental rejection is a key factor. In adolescence, peer rejection and social isolation are also an issue.

Dr. Logan contends that it is not video games that are so much the problem as the isolation that goes with gaming. Better parenting is the key. Children need care, connectedness, consistency and continuity in a healthy context. If the community is not healthy, the context must change so that the community changes or the child is removed to a different context or setting.

From his years of experience in the RCMP, Dr. Logan observed that males account for 80% of violent crime, although the rate of females involved in violent crime is increasing. Trauma experiences or Adverse Childhood Experiences that cause trauma are pervasive, severe, deep, traumatic and life altering. The impact is significant and causes shocking, measurable brain changes. The immune system overreacts. The result to the individual is devastating. Trauma is stored in the body and self-talk will not work.

Early childhood adversity affects the body and health issues later in life. Watch San Francisco pediatrician Dr. Nadine Burke's TED Talk[3] from TEDMED 2014. Dr. Nadine Burke gives specifics on how the body is affected with higher rates of heart disease, cancer, and suicide. High-risk behaviour increases as a result of trauma. Chronic stress and trauma produce PTSD. Ongoing generational sexual trauma produces complex PTSD.

The prerequisite for initiating healing is food, shelter, safety and at least one safe person who can be trusted. Safety is key for addressing trauma. Trauma informed practice is necessary with a holistic approach to reprogram the brain and build new neural pathways. Dr. Nadine Burke shows her program and treatment plan works and she has measurable success in her practice treating trauma (this correlates with Chapter 8: Public Health Crisis).

Municipalities pay the bills for law enforcement and have the power to make the priorities and directives to address human trafficking. Shirley Cuillierier,[4] a Métis, former RCMP commissioner and special advisor on human trafficking to the Federal Public Safety Minister has had over three decades of policing experience and states that crimes to people cost society. From her policing experience she saw that 'survival sex' is not a choice made by women, is not safe and cannot be made safe. Speaking to her, she stressed the importance of a reciprocal relationship between the public and the police. Reporting is critical because without reporting there is no data collection. Without data politicians do not see the problem. Canada needs accurate data with the statistics publicized, so that the public and politicians can recognize the extent of the crime. Laws can then be upheld and strengthened so that human trafficking is addressed in a strategic and organized manner.

The key for law enforcement is to identify victims and deter demand. Law enforcement and service providers have a great deal to teach each other. Service providers are particularly valuable because they have been working with victims for years. Not only police officers on the street but everyone employed at an enforcement agency (including 911 dispatch operators) should learn how to identify a victim of human trafficking. There is a lack of overall training for frontline officers. They do not know what to look for. Law enforcement, service providers and the community must be knowledgeable about human trafficking, its existence, how to help victims and how to bring victims to justice.

Once one victim is found, it is necessary to look for additional victims. Traffickers are always seeking to supply their clients with new, fresh faces. It is important to gather as much information as possible and learn the back-stories of victims. Through restitution orders, money can be seized with the funds transferred to victims and victim services to compensate for the trauma. This is one way that John Schools can be paid for. There is growing evidence that "John Schools" disincentivize criminal behaviour.

John Schools are education programs to stop sex offenders from re-offending. (In Chapter 11, Ed Smith testified about the John Schools he presents to in Saskatchewan). Dr. Michael Shively is the Senior

Advisor on Research and Policy at the National Center on Sexual Exploitation and his research is on the effectiveness of the John School program in the USA.[5]

Effective collaboration occurs when law enforcement works closely with youth workers and frontline service providers. Youth workers see the trends in human trafficking and are an invaluable resource. When I speak with youth workers in the Lower Mainland and Vancouver areas, for example, they tell me that sex trafficking is quickly evolving, and recruitment of ten to twelve-year-old girls is now occurring. There is a similar problem on Vancouver Island.[6] In criminal code language, any person under twelve years of age is considered a child. Youth that are thirteen to nineteen years of age are also being aggressively targeted for the sex industry. Gang recruiting intersects with sex trafficking and has become more organized. The COVID-19 pandemic made it particularly difficult for youth workers to reach youth.

Youth workers say this crime is quickly increasing, spreading and spanning across all communities. It is a much larger problem than politicians and the public are aware. At age sixteen, for example, trafficking victims have typically been in the sex industry for several years and working with them is challenging. The grooming phase can be short, often an overnight. Female recruitment, involving peer-to-peer relationships is more common today and hard drugs are being used to develop dependency.

Youth workers are challenged because often, the youth they are trying to help, are demanding and want something right now. Some youth desire the glamorous lifestyle such as designer handbags, jewellery, and travel, which are initially offered by the traffickers to entice and control young victims. There are few resources to help youth exit the sex industry once they get in. Gangs typically give youth jobs and roles and the youth get street status. Most of these youth are not in school and have not been in school for a long time. Frontline service providers are often not recognizing the signs.

Another missing piece in preventing child abuse and child neglect is that parent support services are lacking. As a result, it is not uncommon for grandparents to be raising grandchildren, particularly in poorer areas and in migrant populations. The pressure and stress on the grandparents are enormous and many lack digital skills for example, so they cannot monitor digital internet activity in the home.

One of the challenges for law enforcement is bridging the barriers against reporting. Law enforcement tell me that the public needs to report, report, report. Without reports, police cannot do anything and exploitation cycles continue.

Youth will rarely report to police on their own. Many fear retaliation from their trafficker or their circle of friends. Traffickers typically manipulate youth into thinking that police are not to be trusted. Youth are threatened that their families will be harmed if they report to police.

Youth reporting to police may not be believed, or nothing is done. On the other hand, I have had experiences with youth and families who have reported and received prompt, professional appropriate help.

Human trafficking is an important crime for law enforcement to understand because human trafficking intersects with all other major crimes. Organized crime groups and transnational syndicates are often involved as is described by survivors in Chapter 11.

Canadian Public Safety Ministry has been providing information webinars on human trafficking. Their third webinar in 2022 was on combating online child sexual exploitation. Law enforcement presenters admitted that there is a worldwide surge in exploitation of children. Officers need a background in technology so there are trained investigators to address the crime. International cooperation is essential because the internet is transnational.

Nationally, there is more proactive law enforcement in some jurisdictions. Edmonton, Winnipeg, Hamilton, Montreal, Halifax, and Toronto have addressed human trafficking for the last several decades. The School Liaison Officer Program is seen as a successful initiative to make students feel safer at school so they can learn better. The Peel Region in the GTA has a proactive, preventative relationship building approach to policing. They focus on creating relationships with mutual respect and they learn to problem solve with the youth. The officers learn skills to engage with the community. In schools, the officers act as deterrents, can respond quickly and de-escalate situations. This reduces the incidents of crime and bullying. With the presence of school liaison officers, school administration and teachers can spend less time dealing with disciplinary matters. The officers can help to deter and de-escalate situations to help students avoid criminal charges.

Internationally there are global best practices in law enforcement. Of particular interest are the officers who are fighting prostitution to enforce the "Equality Model of Law" or Nordic Model in Sweden. The book *Shadow's Law* (2016) by Simon Haggstrom is the true story of a Swedish detective inspector working in Stockholm as head of the Police Prostitution Unit.[7] His book tells the true stories of the people he encountered every day, including the men who buy sex. Haggstrom delved into the back story of each situation to get a thorough understanding of the prostitution culture in Stockholm. This policing approach made his team effective.

"The police are the public and the public are the police; the police being the only members of the public who are paid to give full time attention to duties which are incumbent on every citizen in the interests of community welfare and existence."

SIR ROBERT PEEL (1778–1850)
FOUNDER OF THE LONDON METROPOLITAN POLICE SERVICE

Endnotes

1   Watch Amy's story at covenanthousetoronto.ca/the-problem/sex-trafficking/
2   Dr. Matt Logan, Halo Forensic Behavioural specialists. mattloganhalo.com
3   "How childhood trauma affects health across a lifetime" Dr. Nadine Burke TED Talk, ACEs and childhood trauma. ted.com
4   "RCMP A/Comm. (retired) Shirley Cuillierer receives Governor General's Awards in Commemoration of the Persons Case" BlueLine, Canada's Law Enforcement Magazine, February 26, 2019.
5   endsexualexploitation.org/about/staff/michael-shively/
6   "Human trafficking of teens and tweens a serious issue on Vancouver Island" by Tess van Straaten, Chek News, January 30, 2022.
7   "Shadow's Law" by Simon Haggstrom, Bullet Point Publishing, 2016.

CHAPTER 23

Media

"Whoever controls the media, controls the mind."

JIM MORRISON

Whoever controls the media, controls the culture. Media has a huge influence on our society. On the issue of human sex trafficking, the media in Canada has been largely silent, with the exception of a few articles such as a *Globe and Mail* series by Tavia Grant, and a series by Robyn Doolittle.[1] Both journalists did an exceptional job exposing the world of sexual exploitation in Ontario, but there has been little follow-up.

On the whole, media has supported the pro-prostitution and sex industry lobby, without considering the implications to society, youth, children and the vulnerable. However, it was encouraging to be interviewed by Global News in Manitoba in response to the R vs. Alcorn case, "Manitoba appeals court gives harsher sentence in precedent setting sex trafficking case"[2] by Elisha Dacey, Global News, December 15, 2021 and by Global News television Marney Blunt.

Also, the *Ottawa Hill Times* printed my response to a pro-sex industry article in their paper:

Sex industry wants full decriminalization of prostitution, and that isn't right, writes Peters. July 11, 2022

Regarding the statement: "Laws must be repealed, and sex work must be decriminalized immediately," (The Hill Times, July 4, by Sandra Wesley).

I was a witness for the Protection of Communities and Exploited Persons Act at the House Justice Committee. The law addresses the root cause of harm in prostitution; the buyers of sex (Johns) and profiteers. When this law passed in 2014, the clear statement from Parliament was that girls and women in Canada are not for sale; they are full human beings with dignity and human rights. Full decriminalization of prostitution, which the sex industry wants, communicates the opposite.

The question Canadians need to ask is: do we want more prostitution in Canada or less? I come from Vancouver where the notorious serial killer Robert Pickton illustrated the reality of the sex industry. It's brutal, degrading, and deadly. It is not empowering for any woman or girl. Prostitution relies on human trafficking for recruitment. The vast majority of prostituted people are trafficked or pimped out, and organized crime is typically involved (Dr. Ingeborg Kraus and Scientists for a World Without Prostitution). Moreover, Indigenous women and girls are the first casualties (consider the recent case R vs. Alcorn). With the longest border in the world, Canada would become America's brothel.

Cathy Peters, North Vancouver, B.C.

(The author is a recipient of the Queen's Platinum Jubilee Medal for human trafficking advocacy work and is an anti-human trafficking educator, speaker, and advocate.)

There are small media outlets that will report. Having made presentations to many city councils and regional districts in B.C., local community papers reported on my advocacy work. For example:

- "Students wise up on internet safety: Fernie students have been schooled in ways to protect themselves from child sex traffickers" Kimberley Vlasic, *The Free Press*, April 26, 2018
- "B.C.'s children are at risk, says child sex trafficking watchdog" Sarah Gawdin, *The Abbotsford News*, June 21, 2018
- "The cold reality of global human trafficking" Braden Dupuis, *Pique Newsmagazine*, February 6, 2019
- "Salmon Arm council told 'No community is immune to child sex trafficking'" Martha Wickett, *Penticton Western News*, March 24, 2021
- "Video games one more way to target vulnerable youth" Mike Patterson, *My Cowichan Valley Now*, Thursday, March 25, 2021. A YouTube video presentation accompanies this article on mycowichanvalleynow.com
- "North Cowichan encouraged to help stop sexual exploitation" Robert Barron, *Cowichan Valley Citizen*, March 25, 2021
- "Human trafficking activist visits PRRD" Tom Summer, *Alaska Highway News*, March 26, 2021
- "Human trafficking on city's doorstep campaigner warns White Rock Council" Alex Browne, *Peace Arch News*, April 5, 2021
- "Regional District of Nanaimo asking province to better address human trafficking issue" Karl Yu, *Parksville Qualicum Beach News*, May 16, 2021
- "Williams Lake endorses advocates call for human trafficking task force in BC: Cathy Peters of the Be Amazing Campaign has presented to 87 communities to date" Monica Lamb-Yorski, *Williams Lake Tribune*, May 26, 2021

- "Resolution on sex trafficking passed by NCLGA delegates" Dave Lueneberg, *The Mirror*, May 9, 2022
- "Grand Forks councillor acknowledges sex trafficking as a local problem" Audrey Gunn, *Grand Forks Gazette*, May 11, 2022
- "Anti-human trafficking advocate to speak to CFUW-South Delta" *Delta Optimist*, October 23, 2022

Endnotes

1 "Missing and Murdered: The Trafficked" by Tavia Grant, Globe and Mail, February 10, 2016. "Unfounded: Police dismiss 1 in 5 sexual assaults claims as baseless" by Robyn Doolittle, Globe and Mail, February 3, 2017. theglobeandmail.com
2 "Manitoba appeals court gives harsher sentence in 'precedent-setting' sex trafficking case"by Elisha Dacey, Global News, December 15, 2021. globalnews.ca

CHAPTER 24

Progress

"Be the change."

GHANDI

This issue can be overwhelming, however there is good news; significant progress is being made to expose the crime of human trafficking. The first major step of progress was when human trafficking was recognized as an issue at the United Nations in 2000. The Palermo Protocol[1] was drafted and passed as a universal instrument to "Prevent, suppress and punish trafficking in persons, especially women and children, supplementing the united nations convention against transnational organized crime." Canada ratified this Protocol in 2001.

Of particular interest is Article 9 Section 5 that states "State parties shall adopt or strengthen legislative or other measures, such as educational, social or cultural measures, including through bilateral and multilateral cooperation, to discourage the demand that fosters all forms of exploitation of persons, especially women and children, that leads to trafficking." Discouraging the demand is the key deterrent because it addresses the root cause of the harm, the sex buyer. Sex buyers drive the sex industry where women and girls are dehumanized, degraded, tortured and sexually humiliated in pornography and prostitution.

Progress has occurred with the establishment of the annual TIP or Trafficking in Persons Report by the US State Department. Every year most countries in the world are analyzed for their work to stop human trafficking and the TIP report focuses on concrete, specific actions that governments can take to stop trafficking in their countries. Countries are ranked as Tier One, Tier Two, Tier Two Watch List and Tier Three. Tier One countries are fully compliant with the minimum standards for the elimination of severe forms of trafficking in persons, and Tier Three is not fully compliant and not making significant efforts to be compliant with the minimum standards. Canada is a Tier One country but has significant areas to address.

In the USA, significant progress was made when the State of Rhode Island reversed state law and policies that had allowed the full decriminalization of prostitution for a period of twenty-nine years. The state had benefited from its sex industry for its economic development from 1980 to 2009. Although a few counties in Nevada have legalized prostitution, no other state in the USA has decriminalized prostitution in recent decades. The capital city of Providence in Rhode Island became known as the red-light district of New England. The lack of laws controlling prostitution impeded police from stopping serious crime and arresting traffickers or sex buyers who were acting with impunity. The result in Rhode Island was a significant increase in violence against women, sexual exploitation and slavery. Criminals, organized crime and mainstream businesses exploited women and girls for profit and pleasure. With increased public and police awareness, momentum grew to end the practice of prostitution in Rhode Island. This infamous scenario was documented and researched in detail by Dr. Donna M. Hughes in her academic paper *Decriminalized Prostitution: Impunity for Violence and Exploitation.*[2]

Progress to stop human sex trafficking and sexual exploitation begins when the public recognizes that words are powerful. The sex industry calls prostitution "work" or sex "work" and the public and media have bought in to this line. Sex work and harm reduction language is from the Netherlands where prostitution is fully decriminalized and Germany where prostitution is legalized. The term sex work legitimizes the sex industry, making it palatable and acceptable to the public. Meanwhile there is the need to shift societal attitudes towards recognizing prostitution as inconsistent with equality and human dignity. Reading the preamble to Canada's current law, The Protection of Communities and Exploited Persons Act (Appendix A) helps to understand the intent of the law, which is to protect communities and exploited persons.

There is significant progress as the public becomes more aware about the crime. Any progress will have to be done by individuals, so a nation-wide grassroots movement is needed. This starts with one conversation at a time. This is what I have done in my work; one conversation at a time and each conversation has made a difference.

The most encouraging aspect of my advocacy work has been meeting heroes along the way; the individuals who want to make change. One young man reached out to me by email asking me if he could help me stop the crime of human trafficking. Robert was a high school student on Vancouver Island. He had heard of my advocacy work through his foster mother and reached out to me to ask if he could help. He needed a Social Justice 12 credit and wanted to tackle the difficult issue of human trafficking in British Columbia.

He contacted me in September, which gave him a full school year to learn about the topic before he had to do a final project in the spring. Since I live in the Lower Mainland, we set up a FaceTime session every Monday night for nine months. Robert was in foster care at the time, has cerebral palsy, fetal alcohol syndrome, has lived in a wheelchair his whole life and has overcome tremendous adversity. His final project was to present to Nanaimo city council, which he did exceptionally well.

His familiarity with human trafficking came when a youth from his church group, Mikayla Chang,[3] went missing and was eventually found dead. This case shocked the community in Nanaimo, particularly the youth that knew her. This was a crisis point for Robert, who knew then that he had to do something to stop the crime.

For five years he has presented with me to the general public and professional audiences, culminating in the inaugural global summit called "Stronger Together: Protecting Children from Online Pornography by Inviting a Public Health Response" out of the University of Calgary, Department of Social Work in February, 2022.

Dr. Jocelyn Monsma Selby[4] from the University of Calgary, Department of Social Work, and Liz Walker from Australia (eChildhood) both co-chaired the conference at which Robert and I spoke. These professionals are dedicated to culture-shifting initiatives that equip children and young people. This was the first conference of its kind in the world. In a global summit, we were able to share the dangers and impact of pornography to youth and children. This is progress.

"Change is the end result of all true learning."

LEO BUSCAGLIA

While exploiters have increased in huge numbers, the public is beginning to be aware of the pervasive exploitation taking place in our society. As a result, many not-for-profit organizations are forming to address the problem. More individuals are getting involved to stop the exploitation and to teach and train others to help stop it.

The number of global summits is increasing, involving more global experts and researchers. Collaboration is improving and growing. These important relationships can begin to change the cultural and societal narrative. For example, in Canada two significant summits have begun: the Stronger Together Summit addressing the impact of porn on youth and the Canadian Sexual Exploitation Summit (CSES) sponsored by the NGO, Defend Dignity.

Organizations have promoted important dates; February 22 is National Human Trafficking Awareness Day (Canada), March 8 is International Women's Day, March 8–11 is "Stop Sexual Exploitation of Children and Youth Awareness Week" (British Columbia) and December 2 is "International Day for the Abolition of Slavery." Most recently the United Nations marked November 18 as "World Day for the Prevention of and Healing from Child Sexual Exploitation, Abuse and Violence." As a result, there is progress in bringing sexual exploitation and human trafficking to the attention of the global public.

In Canada significant progress has been made as a result of the PCEPA law. For example, before 2014, 43% of those charged for prostitution were women, whereas by 2022, 90% charged were men. Before PCEPA women were disproportionately charged in prostitution cases. Today, the perpetrators are charged.[5]

For ongoing progress both locally and globally all levels of government must be involved. In my advocacy work in B.C., I am in regular contact with mayors, city councils, regional districts, provincial leaders and federal Members of Parliament. Each level of government has an important role to play, and with consistent collaboration sexual exploitation can be stopped.

Endnotes

1 "Palermo Protocol: Protocol to Prevent, Suppress and Punish Trafficking in Persons Especially Women and Children, supplementing the United Nations Convention against Transnational Organized Crime" Adopted November 15, 2000. Office of the High Commissioner for United Nations Human Rights, OHCHR. ohchr.org

2 "Decriminalized Prostitution: Impunity for Violence and Exploitation" by Dr. Donna Hughes, one of the founders of the academic study of human trafficking. In 2016 she founded the international academic journal "Dignity: A Journal of Sexual Exploitation and Violence." She is a professor and serves as the Director of Graduate Studies in the Gender and Women's Studies Program at the University of Rhode Island. academia.edu

3 "Bacon pleads guilty to lesser murder charge in death of Nanaimo teen Makayla Chang" Nanaimo News Now, August 15, 2022.

4 "Why online porn is a public health issue for kids"by Zoltan Varadi, Faculty of Social Work, September 24, 2021. An interview with Dr. Jocelyn Monsma Selby, a Calgary-based clinical social worker and sexologist specializing in forensic sexology social work. ucalgary.ca

5 "Crimes related to the sex trade: Before and after legislative changes in Canada" www150.statcan.gc.ca

CHAPTER 25

The Laughing Survivor

> "Sometimes when you're in a dark place, you think you've been buried, when actually you've been planted."
>
> CHRISTINE CAINE

Alexandra Stevenson[1] spoke virtually at the Canadian Summit to End Sexual Exploitation (CSES) 2021,[2] when she presented with Kelly Schuler from BRAVE Education for Trafficking Prevention.[3] These two women made a compelling presentation about the importance of prevention education for prepubescent youth aged seven to twelve before they are targeted by the sex industry for exploitation. Alexandra and I have since presented together, and she also presented to the Federal Justice Committee in February 2022.

Alexandra was sex trafficked. Her story is remarkable; because years later with multiple degrees (criminology and psychology) presenting on prevention education, she is able to effectively explain in detail the trauma she endured. She is one of the most effective presenters on sexual exploitation and trafficking in Canada. She calls herself the "Laughing Survivor" because in her quest to understand her own traumatic life experiences she discovered the life saving power of laughter. During her first several years of presenting on sexual exploitation, Alexandra wore her most serious face to tackle the inordinately serious subjects she was surrounded by. And day after day, she worked tirelessly to dismantle the horrors that were happening around her. She quickly found herself getting burnt out.

Understandably, trauma and human trafficking are not considered light-hearted, laughable subjects. Alexandra found that the darkness of these subjects left her without the human connections she so desperately needed to find healing. And while her growing education and experience was helping her understand her trauma, they simply were not providing the light she needed to counteract all that darkness. So, against all odds, she began to laugh.

In the unlikely space that the laughter provided, Alexandra found what she had been looking for; a way to combine her knowledge and education with the human connection that laughter brings. She found that despite the dark subject matter, when she used laughter to punctuate her conversation, she was invited to continue with more conversation. The more people were willing to engage in having these conversations, the more people were educated, and connections formed.

At eleven years of age Alexandra was a bright and engaged child involved in activism. She was sexually assaulted at thirteen and the sexual violence continued through her late teens. She became addicted to drugs. This was a way to deal with the trauma, but it took her down a very different path of life than she had dreamed of following.

She dated drug dealers. She met her boyfriend Chris, who had just gotten out of jail. Alexandra was part of the drug scene when they got together. Chris was not a successful drug dealer and used the drugs he needed to sell. Together they started stealing to buy more drugs. Alexandra thought they had an equal partnership. Because of their money shortage, Chris encouraged Alexandra to start using her body to distract while he stole things. This quickly escalated into Chris physically putting Alexandra up on stage at a strip club, with promises of harm if she did not "make him some money." Chris even sold her to a strip club owner without her having any knowledge of the deal; likely to pay down a drug debt. Alexandra was not a part of the conversation regarding the sale. Chris frequently drugged Alexandra and took pictures of her which he may have traded or sold. Alexandra was not aware of many of Chris' nefarious activities.

When she first started down this path of using her body to make money, she was convinced it was the empowering choice. Having experienced years of both overt sexual assault and covert societal manipulation, she felt that being seen as a sexual object was inevitable and that taking control meant she could at least make money from a situation that felt out of her hands. It wasn't long before any semblance of control she thought she had was gone and she realized the truth, that Chris was and always had been the one in control. Upon this realization, Alexandra made an effort to change her path, but Chris simply did not allow it. He would drug her food and drink at any point he realized Alexandra was trying to use fewer drugs.

The relationship was very violent from the beginning. Her friends were worried, but she did not see it. She said to everyone that she "enjoyed her life," but she was entrenched in a world of exploitation. The reality was she feared for her life.

She overdosed several times and Chris would attack her with everything from threats to knives, to hot lighters. In one fit of rage, he strangled her. She knew that strangulation would kill her but she could not see a way out.

Fortuitously Alexandra was in a car accident, and this gave her a break from Chris for a time. It also gave her a breathing space from doing drugs and to think for herself. She decided she wanted to live differently.

After applying for school and getting accepted to go to Algonquin College for the Child and Youth Worker Program, she moved to Ottawa. Chris was not able to follow her. She did exceptionally well and got straight As. She did so well in school that she applied to the University of Ottawa Bachelor of Social Sciences Honours Criminology program, receiving an entrance scholarship. She loved criminology and loved her schooling for almost two years.

Chris reappeared and her life fell apart. She had to drop out of school due to the stress and anxiety. She went to the police and laid charges against Chris. After going through a lengthy criminal trial, Chris was found not guilty for three out of four of the charges and he was released. The charges were assault causing bodily harm, forcible confinement, uttering death threats and breach of probation. The case was treated as a domestic violence case, with no mention of trafficking.

He found Alexandra shortly after his release and she once again went to the police and began to figure out how to disappear, sure that she would never again have freedom from Chris's harassment and stalking. In a surprise twist of fate, Chris was stabbed to death. Alexandra got her physical freedom. She carried on with her education and got degrees and diplomas but still had to deal with the deep trauma of her past.

The most common question Alexandra is asked: Why did she stay in the relationship with Chris? She finds this a challenging question to answer and admits that every life and situation is different. To begin with Alexandra did not know she was being trafficked. It was far easier to believe she was in control so that she could have an illusion of safety. This idea helped her to survive the constant abuse and violence. When a person experiences ongoing trauma and abuse, they frequently become hard-wired for continued abuse. However, she learned there are two key points: Cognitive dissonance and trauma bonds.

Cognitive dissonance is a state of mental discomfort while doing the thing you hate to do. We have to convince ourselves with the narrative that "I love what I am doing." This protects the victim who is in an impossible situation.

A trauma bond is a very deep attachment, even with those who are hurting us. This is known as the Stockholm Syndrome. Predators are often people we know, and they exploit the vulnerabilities in us. Attachment is the rule not the exception. The bond is created by the perpetrator and accepted by the victim, to have some control. It helps the victim to exist and provides the illusion of safety and control. It helps the survivor to survive. The brain gets used to the ups and downs of the relationship; the good and the bad. Unconsciously the victim will replicate the cycle and they literally blow up their life.

Alexandra explains that child sex trafficking is the exploitation of vulnerability. Traffickers target and prey upon vulnerability. The big problem today, particularly since COVID-19, is that youth feel lonely and isolated. Consequently, they spend too much time online. This makes them vulnerable for predation. Children as young as seven will produce and share inappropriate images. The level of trauma bonding is becoming younger and younger. Sexting is becoming normalized amongst youth, with little understanding of the dangerous consequences.[4] Cutting is increasing because youth are traumatized when they realize their nude photos are online and the photos cannot be retrieved.

There is the trafficking triangle: the buyer, trafficker and seller. The buyer and trafficker are usually men. The seller is usually women and girls (some boys). Alexandra states, "Do not traffic. Do not buy sex. Do not get trafficked." Today, sexual exploitation is everybody's problem because it is a societal problem. Anyone can be a community hero and make a difference. As a society we need to create space for men and boys, so they are taught not to exploit and hurt.

Parents, adults and caregivers need to pay attention to the vulnerabilities of youth. Parents and adults need to talk with youth constantly. We need to teach children about consent, so they understand ownership of their own bodies. We must teach girls to protect themselves, but we need to teach boys that they can use their power and privilege for good. As a society we need to support men to be the best version of themselves. She calls for three important actions:

- Educate yourself;
- Identify vulnerabilities; and,
- Talk.

Build trust with the youth, be consistent, compassionate and use straight talk. Always offer hope because youth need encouragement to believe in a better world. No matter how bad things are it is possible to heal.

Endnotes

1   thelaughingsurvivor.com
2   Canadian Summit to End Sexual Exploitation (CSES). sexualexploitationsummit. ca
3   BRAVE Education for Trafficking Prevention. braveeducation.org
4   National Center On Sexual Exploitation (NCOSE) March 9, 2021. This article on sexting gives statistics and pages of research and bibliography to illustrate potential harm in the digital world. 'Sexting' is the creating, sending, receiving, forwarding of sexually suggestive or explicit texts, photos, or videos via electronic devices and is becoming a common activity among youth. endsexualexploitation.org/articles/2021/03/09

CHAPTER 26

New Zealand

"There is only one word for New Zealand... Epic."

BEAR GRYLLS

My dream in grade six was to visit New Zealand some day. Years later during university years my mother and I traveled there on an around the Pacific Ocean dream trip. In 2015, I took my daughter on a bucket list trip to New Zealand for three wonderful weeks, driving and exploring both islands. We loved the trip. The vast variety, natural beauty, and contrast in landscape on both islands is breathtaking. Every mile we drove we discovered new vistas of volcanoes, verdant valleys, long sandy beaches, spectacular snowy peaks of the South Alps, glaciers, rolling green hills dotted with livestock, waterfalls, river valleys, geothermal springs, and fabulous national parks, making it one of the most beautiful countries in the world.

What saddened us was the evidence of an active sex industry. In Auckland, across from our hotel was a strip club advertising "fresh girls." It was shocking to us that this spectacularly beautiful country of five million people would fully decriminalize the sex industry, turning a blind eye to the evident exploitation of women, girls and the vulnerable.

The New Zealand government passed the New Zealand Prostitution Reform Act (PRA) in 2003. The government was almost completely split on the issue and one vote in favour of the Act, brought it into law for the country. Currently in New Zealand it is legal for any citizen over eighteen years of age to sell sexual services. Brothels and small owner operated brothels (SOOBS) are legal.

The sex industry in Canada cites New Zealand as the best model for addressing prostitution and has pressured the Federal government in Ottawa to repeal the PCEPA Law that criminalizes the buyers of sex and profiteers. The sex industry does not cite the Netherlands and Germany models where full decriminalization and legalization have failed, but chooses the isolated island in the Pacific that has no shared borders. In contrast Canada shares the longest border in the world with the USA. If the current PCEPA law in Canada is repealed, then it becomes possible for Canada to become "America's brothel."

The Trafficking in Persons Report by the USA State Department dropped New Zealand from a Tier One country to a Tier Two country because New Zealand is not fully meeting the minimum standards for the elimination of trafficking. This is a drastic change. To illustrate the New Zealand Model and the problems with it, vcase.ca has produced a short video on their website.[1] Family First in New Zealand wrote a review of the law.[2]

Upon our return, I emailed a letter to the Prime Minister of New Zealand, Jacinta Ardern.

Dear Right Honourable Prime Minister Ardern,

It is an honour to contact you; I have had the privilege to visit New Zealand on two significant and memorable occasions.

The first time was over forty years ago on a once-in-a-lifetime trip with my mother.

The second time was on a once-in-a-lifetime trip with my daughter a few years ago.

We were able to visit the North and South Islands.

Those two visits are highlights in my life.

The difference I saw was concerning; prostitution has become fully decriminalized in New Zealand.

Inadvertently, my daughter and I were booked in a hotel across the street from a strip club (featuring newly arrived girls).

My daughter was shocked, and I was deeply saddened.

Hawaii and Iceland are both stunningly beautiful islands as well; and are popular tourist destinations.

They have chosen to embrace the EQUALITY MODEL (we have it currently in Canada) instead.

They recognize that "modern equal societies do not buy and sell women and children."

My sincere hope is that as Prime Minister you would reconsider the direction of full decriminalization of prostitution and reverse that Law.

My understanding is that brothels in New Zealand are primarily serviced by Maori, Indigenous, Asian and underage youth.

I believe that SOOBS can be anywhere and have no guidelines, transparency, or accountability.

You truly live in one of the most beautiful countries in the world. Full decriminalization of prostitution is not empowering for anyone. It messages to the world that New Zealand is a global sex-tourism destination similar to the Netherlands, Germany, Nevada and Thailand.

This is beyond tragic.

I hope to hear from you.

Sincerely, Cathy Peters

BC anti-human trafficking educator, speaker, advocate

I received a response from the Minister of Justice who explained the stance of the government supporting full decriminalization of prostitution. I then emailed every Member of Parliament in New Zealand and received some letters of support.

Endnotes

1   "Prostitution and Human Trafficking in New Zealand - Aotearoa" A video short by VCASE on prostitution and human trafficking in New Zealand. vcase.ca
2   "Is it Working? An Evidenced-Based Review of the Decriminalisation of Prostitution in New Zealand" familyfirst.org.nz

CHAPTER 27

Global Initiatives

"Something must be done, and 'something' is that men must learn to live virtuously."

JOSEPHINE BUTLER
GREAT BRITAIN, 1896

*Instrumental in the campaign to raise the age of consent
from twelve to sixteen to protect girls from sexual abuse.*

The crime of human trafficking has been recognized as the fastest growing crimes in the world and one of the most lucrative. Joy Smith is considered Canada's authority on human trafficking. The global representative and special advisor on human trafficking is Valiant Richey with the Organization for Security and Cooperation of Europe (OSCE).[1] Valiant worked in Seattle as Chief Prosecutor and was successful in stemming the sex trade in Seattle and King County. His work became recognized globally and he trained law enforcement and prosecuting teams from around the world.

As a global initiative his work is groundbreaking because he focused on stopping the harm in prostitution by stopping the sex buyers from buying sex. He presented in Vancouver to both law enforcement and to frontline service providers in 2017. The recent OSCE report that he facilitated is called "Discouraging Demand"[2] and outlines a strategy that is recognized as the only effective way to significantly deter prostitution.

He begins his presentations[3] with a quote from former prostitute and author Rachel Moran, "How do you expect to uproot a tree when all you do is rip at the leaves." Valiant is determined to deter the commercial sex industry because of its rampant exploitation. From data and research his team discovered it is a crime of power and privilege that punishes the vulnerable and rewards the privileged. Ultimately human trafficking crushes minority populations and vulnerable communities experience tremendous harm. He states that unless the demand is targeted, the commercial sex industry will continue to flourish. Demand drives the exploitation. If there are no buyers, there is no business.

The full decriminalization of prostitution that the sex industry is aggressively pushing for would embolden a much larger buyer's market. The question becomes where does the supply come from? With globalization victims are moved around the world typically from developing countries to developed countries. From a human rights perspective, how can this be acceptable?

The Seattle/King County Model is similar to the Equality Model in Canada that recognizes the steps needed to assist exploited persons and to provide deterrents for exploiters.

For exploited persons:
- Reduce involvement in the system.
- Safe harbour and mandatory diversion for children.
- Diversion and meaningful alternative service for adults.
- Affirmative defense.
- No convictions.
- Online victim outreach.

For exploiters:
- Prevention
- Disruption
- Intervention
- Accountability

His experience—thirteen years as Crown Prosecutor in Seattle and current work as human trafficking advisor for the OSCE—has shown that there is no universal type of victim. All demographics and socioeconomic categories are represented and there is no single method of entry. Entry can be via a boyfriend, through abduction, social media, drug addiction or poverty. The one commonality is that most victims are vulnerable; 75% to 95% are abused as children. Pimps control 90% of prostituted persons. Most are recruited between twelve to fourteen years of age and disproportionately, they are from minorities and ethnic groups.

His experience discovered pimping is predatory, but overwhelmingly pimps or traffickers are businessmen. The business goal is to make money. Not all traffickers are psychopathic, although they are sadistic. They consider their work purely in economic terms.

The scope of the problem is dramatically increasing. In the USA as an example, 100,000 to 300,000 children are trafficked and up to 70% of the street youth are victims.

As a strategy, Valiant Richey's team in Seattle/King County initially went after the traffickers, because that was the status quo for law enforcement in the USA. However, Valiant Richey learned that if the ultimate goal is to end commercial exploitation, the buyers of sex must be prosecuted. Buyers of sex or johns have become more violent, deviant and much more dangerous. The prevalence of violence in commercial sex buying is deeply traumatic for the seller who is the victim. For example, Valiant's team discovered 73% of victims are physically assaulted, 64%

to 83% are threatened with a weapon, 50% to 60% are raped, 90% want out of The Life.

Arrested buyers are usually found to have purchased sex more than once. Universally, there was heavy pornography use. In turn, there is a high prevalence of violence in sex buying. The buyers come from all professions and are executives, pastors, teachers, lawyers, tech experts, labourers. He found that typically the buyers in King County were from a white middle upper class background buying minorities who were poor and disadvantaged.

This demonstrates that it is an issue of power and privilege.

To confirm Valiant Richey's observations is the research by Steve Grubman Black[4] who concludes with, "A John is a man who believes he is entitled by virtue of his gender and money to have sex on demand. Whether he is shy or not, whether he calls her a girlfriend or a whore, and whether or not he abides by some set of rules or limits, he believes he can buy for sexual use a woman's body." The father, an uncle or other adult male identity figure, had taken a number of the sex buyers that Grubman Black interviewed, to a prostitute when they were younger. This first sexual experience made a lasting impression on them and established in their minds that women are second-class citizens that can be bought and used in this way.

In his presentations Valiant Richey gives examples of strategies to successfully address demand. For example:

1. John Schools

The King County prosecuting team tried traditional buyer stings, but they were not catching enough offenders and were not catching the worst offenders. The penalties were low, the resources were low, and the underlying networks were not being addressed. When Valiant Richey was working in King County there were 38 police agencies, and they established a buyer intervention program called 'John Schools.' The court referred the buyers and the johns had to pay for it. The program was ten weeks. The county paid nothing for the program. The buyers paid a fine, which covered the services, and the program was open to self-referral as well. This has been successful in the john schools. Most buyers admitted they did not enjoy buying sex but got in a cycle, they were stuck in. Sex buyers admitted why they would stop:

- Tired of the lies and secrets.
- Tired of spending the money.
- Does not want to lose wife or family.
- Did not understand the harm they were causing.
- Felt it was not right.
- Does not want daughter, sister, mother to know.

Buyers need viable programs to help them stop buying sex.

2. Technology

Another strategy that Richey has used is to disrupt searches that target buying the women and girls for sex. The most common action is for buyers to click through online ads at 2:00 pm while at work to set up a date after work. It is estimated 40% to 70% of men who access porn are at work. This affects the workplace and contributes to depression, anxiety and exhaustion. As a result, the King County prosecuting team ran an ad campaign on the search sites to offer help for the buyers to stop the cycle of purchasing sex. This is a form of "buzz-kill" and intercepted the transaction before the buyer made the purchase. It is online deterrence, and humorous ads were the most effective. Surprisingly the team found that a growing number of buyers were young, and the ad campaign was especially effective in reaching the eighteen to twenty-four age group.

The key is to target young men to get into their heads about what they are doing so they would think twice before buying sex.

3. Employers

Since a high prevalence of sex buyers are at work and employed by reputable organizations, employers can have considerable leverage over their employees by having clear expectations of computer use. It has become more common for employees to use company time to book dates, view pornography and even meet sellers on the employer's property. Businesses care about this issue of commercial sex buying because it becomes a liability and causes loss of productivity.

4. Education

High schools and middle schools must teach the importance of respect, empathy, integrity, mutuality in addition to understanding the crime of trafficking. Universities need to address sexual assault and domestic violence on campuses and incorporate commercial sex discussion. In King County, a local university had some of the largest number of buyers for underage girls. Prevention education shifts attitudes. Sexual exploitation is gender-based violence, but the gender causing the violence is not being addressed. Therefore, the problem is not getting better. There is an opportunity here for education and focus on men and boys. The need is for sustained broad prevention programs.

5. The Targets

Protect marginalized populations because these groups are vulnerable, and some have no one else who cares for them. The worst example was the Green River killer Gary Ridgeway who targeted fifty juvenile prostitutes.

6. Health Sector

The most overlooked sector and yet this crime has serious public health implications. The health sector has a lot of interaction with buyers because buyers get their STI testing at doctor clinics. Sellers, the victims, often end up in the emergency room for treatment. He advises the use of the Violence Prevention Model as opposed to the ineffective Harm Reduction Model.

7. Media

Media has created a culture war by glamorizing the sex industry and inadvertently aggravating exploitation. The media needs to understand the harm of sex buying and prostitution. Media can be very effective in raising public awareness in order to shame the practise of sex buying.

The keys to make these strategies effective are to build public awareness, create cultural change and rebuild constructive attitudes. Valiant Richey stresses the need for the public to partner with law enforcement and their needs to be province, state-wide and local alliances between the public and police.

Valiant Richey describes the girls and young women that need treatment and help to get out of the sex industry. He emphasizes that to exit the sex industry, transition houses are needed. They can be small, but need to be safe, secure and supportive. Rehabilitation is very expensive and there needs to be a strong business plan, good funding and the ability to connect with the community. It will often take seven or eight points of intervention before someone will choose help and exit the sex industry. Girls are typically looking for touch points of family. The key is to give the girls the ability to choose and develop the skills to create a healthy future.

The sex buyer creates deep physical and emotional harm, and victims suffer greatly. A root problem for these vulnerable women and girls is child abuse. Once a woman is healed and her trauma addressed, she can improve and begin to slowly heal. Girls that are exiting, must learn basic life skills. Many girls have a low reading level and need educational skills and tools. Learning to manage finances, have driving lessons, find careers or starting back in school are all important life skill steps. Some innovative programs offer puppy, art and equine therapy. Many offer parenting training. Many girls have requested tattoo removal. I know a dentist who offers his services for free to repair the teeth of survivors. Long-term drug use damages teeth, and this is one service that girls in recovery deeply appreciate.

Survivors have typically never experienced a healthy way of life, having entered prostitution at twelve to fourteen years of age, developing trauma bonding and low self-esteem. Most have experienced extreme abuse causing severe dysfunction in their childhoods, have run away, and used drugs to numb the pain.

To find boundaries, the girls will initially push limits in every way. To survive, they have learned to be extreme manipulators. It can take months for them to learn to dream again. Consistent patience, care and love is critical. They have experienced severe trauma and specialized trauma treatment is needed. The first step is detox.

Finding skilled trained compassionate staff is challenging, and staff must have clear boundaries to work with survivors. Many remarkable committed individuals have taken on this work. They are willing to do onerous work yet receive little gratitude. They do the work because they see the need, the value and potential in each girl. Rehabilitative services are needed for boys as well, and generally there is a severe shortage of these facilities in Canada and globally.

Valiant Richey now works for the much larger agency of the OSCE and tracks global trends of human trafficking by collecting data, doing on the ground research and writing strategy reports and guidelines for the fifty-seven countries within the OSCE. He speaks internationally and encourages countries to follow through on their international commitments.

An initiative that the OSCE created was the International Survivors of Trafficking Advisory Council or ISTAC.[5] Twenty-one survivors represent ISTAC from fourteen different countries. Their global concern is that less than one percent of trafficking is detected, and the problem globally is getting worse rapidly. Traffickers are innovative, organized, sophisticated and constantly adopting new ways to lure and groom women and girls into the sex industry. COVID-19 has worsened the situation and traffickers use the internet effectively to target vulnerable victims.

This council of survivors insist that it is very important to distinguish between trafficking survivors who speak about their needs and rights versus the organizations that promote the development of the sex trade.

Trisha Baptie from B.C., and Tamea Nagy from Ontario, represent Canada as survivors at the ISTAC. Valiant Richey and the OSCE team recognize the importance of victim survivor voices that needs to be at the forefront of anti-human trafficking strategies. A global survivor's network is invaluable for advice and guidance to the global community. This council is victim centred using a survivor and human rights based approach. The council recognizes that focusing on the demand, the buyers, is fundamental and paramount to address and discourage trafficking. As an example, in 1999, Sweden, the most egalitarian country in the world, was the first country to charge buyers. This has proven to be a meaningful deterrent, effectively transforming Sweden's societal norms into a model of gender equality.

Along with Valiant Richey in Europe, Dr. Ingeborg Kraus from Germany is internationally recognized. She is a trauma therapist (Chapter 8) who has worked in war-torn countries with sexually traumatized women and girls. She speaks publicly and is the initiator of the Public Appeal of Trauma Therapists for a World Without Prostitution. Her website is "Trauma and Prostitution."[6] She works with sexual assault and prostituted victims and documents their stories. Her research is well known and well received because she has worked with hundreds of victims and documented their cases. She has become an important voice for the voiceless. Her two articles, *Prostitution and choice* in 2014, and *Trauma as the pre-condition and consequence of prostitution* in 2016, are thorough descriptions of the harm of prostitution. Dr. Kraus submitted a brief to the Canadian Federal Justice Committee in February 2022. In her brief she makes important points:

- Germany's liberal prostitution policy has contributed to an explosion of the demand and an increase in violence against women in prostitution. It amounts to a collective degradation of women across society. It operates as a catalyst for forced prostitution, pimping and human trafficking and has made Germany into the brothel of Europe.
- Prostitution destroys people. Prostitution is serious violence.
- To call prostitution "work" is to cover up the violence.
- Prostitution is neither work nor an opportunity.

In the United States, there are sizable NGOs that have global influence, such as the National Centre on Sexual Exploitation (NCOSE) with executive director Dawn Hawkins, Shared Hope International[7] with executive director and former Congress woman Linda Smith and the International Justice Mission[8] with CEO Gary Haugen. These organizations rescue victims, educate the public, train service providers, fund lawsuits, recommend public policy and legislation, and organize global conferences. Each of these organizations is proficient and effective. They have informative websites where their activities are listed. It is a huge benefit to have these organizations; they offer exceptional timely resources for the readers. These organizations believe that it is essential to raise awareness, address the demand and supply side, while upholding the rights of victims and maintaining victim protection as a priority.

Shared Hope International compiles an annual state by state report card, ranking every state in the USA according to how well they are addressing child sexual exploitation. This report card has created incentive for policy and lawmakers to carefully review the crime and strategies in their respective states. It has helped to move the dial forward in addressing the crime in the USA. Shared Hope International highlights four strategies:

- Eliminate demand.
- Prosecute traffickers.
- Identify victims.
- Provide protection for victims, access to services, shelter for victims.

Addressing youth issues and internet challenges, there are three effective NGOs in the USA: Defend Young Minds[9] with Kirsten Jensen, Protect Young Eyes[10] with Chris McKenna and Parents Against Child Abuse[11] with Tania Haigh. These NGOs are doing exemplary work in educating parents about the dangers children face today in a digital world. Their websites and blogs are full of current up to date strategies with keys and tips for raising healthy resilient children. Kirsten Jensen, Chris McKenna and Tania Haigh give presentations regularly at the global summits on sexual exploitation and are available to give presentations virtually and in person.

In the USA, the Polaris Project[12] is a leading data-driven social justice movement fighting sex and labour trafficking. They service the national wide Human Trafficking Hotline number in the USA (1-888-373-7888). Consequently, they can gather data on this crime.

The National Center for Missing & Exploited Children (NCMEC)[13] in the USA, founded in 1984, is the nation's largest child protection organization. Their goal is to protect children, provide resources, and the Center gives important data and statistics on the problem. They have circulated millions of photos of missing children and assisted law enforcement in the recovery of more than 376,000 missing children. Their number is 1-800-THE-LOST.

The NCMEC also operates a tip line for reporting Child Sexual Abuse Material (CSAM). In 2021, the Cybertip line received over 29 million reports, up from 21 million reports in 2020. This is an increase of more than 40% in one year. The tip line received more than ten times the number of reports than a decade ago. Child sexual abuse material is evolving, becoming more and more egregious. To counter the problem the NCMEC offers an online safety program called NetSmartz.[14] They emphasize a basic principle, "Tell children that when you put a photo out there, you cannot get it back. The person you think you are talking to may not be that person."

Dr. Melissa Farley founded Prostitution Research Education[15] out of San Francisco in 1995. It is a not-for-profit organization conducting research on prostitution, pornography and human trafficking. It offers education and consultation to researchers, survivors, the public and policymakers. Dr. Farley has done ground-breaking research in Vancouver, B.C. She has written books including *Prostitution, Trafficking, and Traumatic Stress* where she identifies the extreme and pervasive forms of trauma involved in prostitution, exploitation and trafficking.

In her presentations she states that "prostitution is where trafficking happens, and prostitution is where pornography happens." From her decades of research, she notes that children and adults are at different points in the same continuum of abuse. Power imbalance between the buyer and seller of sex is the problem. In a conversation, she pointed out to me that the pipeline to prostitution is twofold: child abuse including incest and unchecked pornography.

Another organization that has excellent teaching videos, Exodus Cry,[16] produces documentaries and presents to Federal and International Committees examining Human Trafficking.

The organizations and individuals mentioned above are doing excellent work but with the rapid growth of the sex industry, much more needs to be done.

"Too often efforts are only focused on victim identification or the prosecution of traffickers. If we don't address demand (the sex buyers) the problem will never, never stop."
—*Valiant Richey, Special Advisor to the OSCE, Austria*

"There is not a single one of the established political parties that has set out a human rights-based solution to the hell on earth that is the German prostitution system."
—*Dr. Ingeborg Kraus, Ph.D. Psychology, internationally renowned psychotraumatologist, Germany*

"Question to the sex buyer: I met many of you. So many. Too many. And I always wondered about you. I wondered how could you justify this to yourself? How could you tell yourself—and believe it—that I was happy to have strangers' fingers, penises and tongues shoved into the most private parts of

me? How did you convince yourself that I'd be happy about something you'd never, in your wildest nightmares, wish on your own daughter? I wondered, most of all, how could you look at me and not see me?"

—Rachel Moran, who was in prostitution in Dublin from the age of fifteen to twenty-two years, and author of 'Paid For: My Journey Through Prostitution', Ireland

Endnotes

1 Valiant Richey is the Organization for Security and Cooperation in Europe (OSCE) Special Representative and Co-ordinator for Combating Trafficking in Human Beings. He represents the OSCE at the political level on anti-trafficking issues, and assists the 57 OSCE participating states in the development and implementation of anti-trafficking strategies and initiatives.

2 "Discouraging the demand that fosters trafficking for sexual exploitation" Organization for Security and Cooperation in Europe (OSCE), June 10, 2021. This paper puts a spotlight on the role of demand in encouraging exploitation and causing harm to victims. The primary aim of the paper is to support and enhance the implementation of state-led responses to demand.

3 It is worth watching the teaching and speaking videos by Valiant Richey. He also presents regularly for the OSCE and at Global Summits such as the NCOSE Annual Summit: "Demand for Human Trafficking: We are all responsible as consumers—how can we end this cycle?" June 2022. vimeo.com
"What about the Buyers? Fighting Human Trafficking by Fighting Demand" December 2021. youtube.com
"Why We Must Address Demand to End Trafficking" World Without Exploitation Webinar, June 2020. vimeo.com
"Timber! Strategies for uprooting Commercial Sexual Exploitation" NCOSE Conference, May 2018. vimeo.com
"Truth about Porn" Valiant Richey Interview, November 2018. vimeo.com
"Part 2: Ending Commercial Sexual Exploitation, Q&A with Valiant Richey" June 2019. vimeo.com

4 Steve Grubman Black, "Deconstructing John" Demand Dynamics Conference, DePaul University, Chicago, Illinois, October 16, 2003. Black is known for his book "Broken Boys/Mending Men: Recovery from Childhood Sexual Abuse" Blackburn Press, 2002. ISBN-10-1930665628

5 ISTAC: International Survivors of Trafficking Advisory Council, January 25, 2021. osce.org

6 Dr. Ingeborg Kraus. trauma-and-prostitution-eu/
"Trauma as the Pre-Condition and Consequence of Prostitution" by Sandra Novak, November 6, 2016. sandranovak.com

7 Shared Hope International. sharedhope.org

8 International Justice Mission. ijm.ca

9 defendyoungminds.com

10 protectyoungeyes.com

11 paxa.online

12 Polaris Project operates the National Hotline Number for Human Trafficking, USA. polarisproject.org

13 National Center for Missing & Exploited Children (NCMEC). missingkids.org

14 NetSmartz. netsmartzkids.org

15 Dr. Melissa Farley. Founder of Prostitution Research Education. prostitutionresearch.com

16 Exodus Cry. exoduscry.com

CHAPTER 28

What Can You Do?

"Do what you can with what you have where you are."

ROOSEVELT

A simple strategy for addressing sexual exploitation is: Learn. Share. Alert. Learn about the issue and crime. It is important to educate yourself about the issue. Look out for the warning signs and any red flags. Do you have a gut feeling something is "off?" Be aware of online activities of youth.

Share what you learn with family, friends and your sphere of influence. Share with the youth in your life. Connect with service providers so you know what help is available. Then share the resources with your contacts.

Alert local politicians and police because they have the power to do something.

Here is a partial list of what I encourage the public to do:
- Educate yourself about the issue.
- Know the warning signs and human trafficking indicators.
- Look up online: beamazingcampaign.org, vcase.ca, and joysmithfoundation.com
- Skim articles on peer-reviewed journal website: Dignity: A Journal on Sexual Exploitation and Violence.[1]

- Share what you learn with someone.
- Raise awareness.
- Know your community resources.
- Watch videos and set up an internet search alert to receive news on the topic.
- Think globally. Act locally.
- Report any suspicious human trafficking activities to police.
- Call for change: email, call or write a letter to leaders (civic, provincial, federal) to ask them to address the problem of human trafficking, sexual exploitation, youth and child exploitation in your community by focusing on the education of the public and enforcement of the law. Template letters can be found at vcase.ca.
- Ask the local police what they know about the issue and what they are doing about it.
- Support anti-human trafficking policies and support exit programs for trafficked women.
- Promote prevention education programs.
- Share Canada's hotline number and order posters, postcards and wallet cards from the CCTEHT and distribute these in your community.
- Take a stand. The goal for girls: to be strong and confident. For boys: to be respectful.
- Girls: talk to your father, brothers, boyfriend and family about the reality of women and girls being exploited in the sex industry.
- Boys: do not pay for sex or go to places where commercial sex acts take place either here or abroad.
- Share your concerns with others.
- Talk about the issue of objectification of women and girls; that it is a human rights issue.

- Help the heroes: volunteer and help frontline workers, NGOs (Non-Government Organizations) and the organizations that help survivors of human trafficking.
- Fundraise for NGOs.
- Watch documentaries *Enslaved and Exploited* and *Red Light, Green Light* by Jay and Michelle Brock, two Canadian filmmakers.
- Watch films *Childhood 2.0*, *I Am Jane Doe*, *Our Kids Online: Porn, Predators and How to Keep them Safe*
- Read *Invisible Chains* by UBC law professor Benjamin Perrin, *The True Story of Canadian Human Trafficking* by Paul Boge, *Sex Industry Slavery, Protecting Canada's Youth* by Dr. Robert Chrismas.
- Take the online course on Human Trafficking from B.C. OCTIP (Office to Combat Trafficking in Persons).
- Watch TED Talks by survivors Trisha Baptie and Casandra Diamond.
- Study the effect of porn on the developing brain (neuroscience research) by Dr. Gary Wilson.[2]
- Watch the Dr. Jackson Katz TED Talk on men, violence and silence.
- Check out prevention websites such as Fight the New Drug, Defend Young Minds, Protect Young Eyes, Parents Against Child Abuse.
- Review "Top Issue" pages on the NCOSE (National Center On Sexual Exploitation) website: Child Sexual Abuse, Pornography, Prostitution Sex Buying, Sex Trafficking, Sexual Violence.
- Understand the effects of internet use, its strengths and weaknesses.
- Take a cyberspace safety education course and share what you learn with your family.
- Research how to be safe online and share that information with your family.

- Build and stay connected with a supportive family and community network.
- Have mentors; be a mentor.
- Develop interests that get you involved and contributing to the community where you live.
- Attend a global summit, for example "Coalition to End Sexual Exploitation Online Global Summit" put on by NCOSE (USA) or the Canadian Sexual Exploitation Summit. These are virtual and free. They provide current research, data, resources, and networking opportunities.

Endnotes

1   digitalcommons.uri.edu/dignity
2   "Your Brain on Porn" by Dr. Gary Wilson. Commonwealth Publishing, 2014. ASIN: BOON2AH8NW

CHAPTER 29

For Parents, For Youth

"Everybody needs four things in life: something to do, someone to love, something to hope for, and someone to believe in."

LOU HOLTZ

For parents, the key is to have age-appropriate conversations so their youth can develop their own internal filter about pornography and healthy sexuality. These conversations need to start early and be ongoing.

Youth today are experiencing pressure to be sexualized like never before. Parents need to be aware and pro-active. For example, sexting has become normalized, and parents are often not aware of it.[1] Sexting, as we saw in the Amanda Todd case (Coquitlam, November 2022) can lead to cyber bullying. It is also important for parents to be aware of online dating apps and the growing popularity of online relationships. As a result, dating has become more susceptible to compromising situations. With the normalization of pornography, viewing the world of interpersonal relationships has become a confusing complex experience for youth today.

A simple strategy for parents:
- Address the topic of pornography with your children.
- Explain the boyfriending tactic of grooming for sex trafficking.
- Teach and role model healthy relationships.

Working in this space for over forty years, teaching at risk youth as a high school teacher, becoming a parent, and presenting on this issue for years has taught me that a parent is a child's main influencer. Parents need to role model healthy relationships and talk about sexuality to their children. While many parents are discouraged and do not think they have influence in their child's life, they are the main influencers. Runaway and throwaway youth have told frontline service providers and me that they wished they had a loving mom and dad. Youth and children seek authenticity, and simply want to be loved. Parenting today is a challenge, but there is a simple adage: be firm, be fair and be fun.

Josh Shipp is a teen behaviour expert.[2] He speaks to the very difficult issues of sexting, porn use, and cutting (self-harm). His online talks amplify these messages:
- **What you don't talk out, you will act out.** He is referring to the importance of youth speaking up.
- **We don't see you as a problem, we see you as an opportunity.** This is the line that his foster parents stated to him when he first arrived at their home.
- **Every child is one decision away from success or failure.** This is an encouragement to educators and parents.
- **Every child is one caring consistent adult away from being a success story.**
- **Every child who winds up doing well has had at least one stable and committed relationship with a supportive stable adult.**
- **Be your best.** His call to youth.

- **Choose; be bitter or better.** His challenge to youth.
- **Young people want to succeed and do well, and it is not what you say, but how you say it.** His challenge to parents.

Cutting is becoming more common and is a sign of trauma reaction. On cutting, Josh shares with parents, not to overreact and to ask the following questions: Be direct. "What is hurting you and causing you pain?" As a parent, find something to replace the cutting and get therapy for the youth.

Regarding porn viewing, Josh suggests not to take on this issue face-to-face but to go for a drive or hike. Ask, "What do you know and think about porn?" Explain to your youth that porn addiction is a real and dangerous thing. Porn is damaging because people become objects. Porn is a fantasy. It will damage relationships and future marriage. Youth are looking at pornography to get their sex education. Porn is targeting youth aggressively through porn sites even by masquerading as sexual wellness centres.

Do not use guilt or shame but educate. After a difficult conversation, go and get ice cream! Do something fun. Alexander Stevenson, the Laughing Survivor (Chapter 25), shared with me many strategies that parents can use to connect with their children. First, it is very important for parents to understand what human trafficking is. While the definition is clear, the crime itself is insidious, subtle and coercive. Youth and children can be trafficked without knowing it. Sexual assault or incest can set the children up for ongoing abuse later and is often the precursor to prostitution.

Parents need to traffic-proof their children. How is this done? Start conversations early. Teach the concept of consent to young children so they understand they have control of their bodies. Teach them critical learning skills. Talk kindly, consistently and constantly. Give your children permission to talk to you anytime about any subject. Silence helps predators while conversations help everyone. Children today are particularly vulnerable and can easily get misinformation from peers and the internet. They frequently lack education yet have easy access to online forums.

Dr. Gail Dines cites some warning signs:
- Withdrawal from family, peers, activities.
- Closes devices when the parent enters the room.
- Spends excessive time in the bathroom.
- Secretive about online/offline friends.
- Lack of sleep.
- Uses precocious sexual language.
- Mood shifts, depression, anxiety.
- Excess money and expensive products.

Dr. Pam Chapman, a licensed clinical social worker (LCSW) from the US gave me specific advice for parents. She recognizes that today's hyper-sexualized culture has made parenting very challenging. The goal is to raise healthy, resilient youth. There are huge risks now with the internet and parents must be vigilantly aware about what is going on.

While it takes a village to raise a child, it is important to vet that village carefully. Know the teachers and leaders involved with your children. What are they teaching? Go regularly to parent/teacher meetings for example.

Ask your children what they are learning about. Volunteer in their classroom. Get a list of the books and videos your children are getting exposed to. Meet with the principal to find out policies and protocols for online safety. Predatorial behaviour from peers and from staff in schools is becoming more common, so find out the policy for administration and staff to protect children.

Children listen and watch. It is important for parents to live the lifestyle they want their children to live. Positive healthy role models are key. Get extended family as involved as possible but vet them first.

Parents need to know what is going on. Develop traditions and family experiences that ground your children, so they feel secure and loved. Are your children safe at home? If not, get family therapy so there is help and support. Self-care for parents is important. Parents need support as well. There are lots of free support programs available.

Who are your children hanging out with? You need to know your children's friends and their families. You need to know who they spend time with and who they listen to. Who influences them?

Do you have computer and phone protocols and strategies in place for all family members? Do your children know what these are? Children online can find themselves in very dangerous situations and not know how to handle them. Youth and children need guidance.

Find out the interests and passions of your children. What are their interests and abilities? Encourage your children in these and find suitable activities that match their interests.

Innocent Lives Foundation[3] gives the following suggestions to protect children from predation with acronym TRUST:
• Talk about what influences them.
• Relationships- teach what healthy relationships look like.
• Understand empathy to reach youth.
• Stability and consistency- maintain these.
• Teach about grooming, boundaries and how to report.

A child, who is actively involved in school, participates in healthy activities, has drug-free role models and who lives a healthy lifestyle, can learn to say "No" to peer pressure. Parents need to understand the importance of discipline, regular routines and attentive care in the use of social media.

The most important thing that parents can do is to take time with their children and share their wisdom with their children. Shared life lessons are invaluable and produce positive legacies. Give youth something solid to stand on so they have a strong sense of self-worth. A strong family is a huge asset for any child. A strong family will role model well, show the way to live well, and give the skills to children so they can learn to live independently.

A healthy family will teach healthy coping skills and will start with a positive narrative. Healthy relationships are exemplified by care, consideration, respect, mutuality, honesty, integrity, kindness and love. Youth need to be taught that love and sex are not the same thing.

We want children to function at their highest level. Come alongside your children and be their cheerleaders. Be there emotionally and physically. Ask questions. Be concerned.

Dr. Micheal Gurian[4] is a family counsellor and author of over thirty books. He speaks on violence against women and has done research on the "boy crisis" in America. One of his best-selling books is *Saving Our Sons; A New Path for Raising Healthy and Resilient Boys.*

Regarding raising boys Dr. Gurian makes three points:
- Talk and talk and talk with him. When boys discover they are worthy of respect and understanding, they learn to respect and empathize with others.
- Foster his respect for others. Respect for ourselves feeds our respect for others. Set goals and expectations and live up to them. Teach responsibility by having him participate in chores at home. Teach him how to relate well to family and friends so he can become a

reflective, conscious-centred adult with a strong sense of identity and moral fibre.

- Find good role models, both male and female. Teach him to respect his mother and he will respect other women and girls. Sport superstars, coaches, tutors, babysitters, extended family members, even fictional characters or heroes of the past can give a boy role-models to emulate.

Dr. Gurian states we need to instill in our boys virtues of integrity, honesty, truthfulness, goodness, self-control, kindness, empathy, generosity, problem-solving, optimism, perseverance, respect for others, compassion and respectfulness. The question for a boy or son is, "Are you giving your best? Does that activity help you become your best? Does it make others better and their best? Are you hurting or helping? Is that the right thing to do?"

Dr. Gurian states the Golden Rule, "Treat others the way you want to be treated" to get boys to think about their behaviour and the consequences of their behaviour.

Dr. Michele Borba[5] is an educational psychologist who asks similar types of questions and who encourages youth to study great moral leaders and heroes. She encourages youth to stand up for what is right, true and good reminding them that this takes courage. Seven character strengths she says are important for healthy development are integrity, self-control, empathy, self-confidence, optimism, perseverance, and curiosity. She encourages parents to raise unselfies, not selfies. Recently from her research she sees empathy skills dipping and narcissism rising in our culture. She encourages families to develop habits of the heart. Have close, personal moments. Empathy needs to be now, real and spontaneous. Empathy is intentional and will transform us. Empathy starts with one person and makes us better people. Empathy is about us, not me.

Dr. Borba is very concerned about the rise in sexual violence.[6] Regarding porn viewing and sexual exploitation, her concluding question is, "Would you want your sister or any family member experiencing that?"

Safewise.com addresses family safety issues.[7] Lead reporter Rebecca Edwards wrote *How to Keep Your Teen (or Tween) Safe Online*, October 21, 2021. She lists the top online threats for teens:

- Cyberbullying.
- Sexting.
- Identity theft by cybercriminals.
- Pornography, which creates unrealistic expectations, low self-esteem and confuses a teenager's understanding of romantic relationships.
- Online predators, who pose as peers to connect with potential victims.

She offers tips to keep teens safe online:
- Talk about it. Communication is key.
- Set up ground rules in the home for online use.
- Keep devices and computers in a central place where you can monitor activity and enforce boundaries. Set limits for screen time.
- Put protections in place.
- Know your teen's social network profiles.
- Look for signs of trouble: secretive behaviour, creating new email accounts, self-harm, becoming sullen or withdrawn, losing interest in friends or activities, displaying strong emotional responses after going online.

To conclude on a positive note, youth tell me consistently that the most important information they want to know is how to have healthy relationships. What does a healthy relationship look like? Cybertip.ca does an excellent job on their website section under resources, describing signs of a healthy relationship versus an unhealthy relationship. For example, healthy relationships will exhibit kindness, courtesy, consideration, thoughtfulness, trust, respect, honesty, reliability, equality, communication, appreciation and acceptance. These shared qualities develop emotional closeness and connection.

Endnotes

1 jonnyshannon.com/blog/the-ugly-truth-about-sexting
2 joshshipp.com/teen-behavior-help
3 Innocent Lives Foundation. innocentlivesfoundation.org
4 Dr. Michael Gurian, author of over 30 books and marriage and a family counsellor. He addresses the boy crisis in America. michaelgurian.com
5 Dr. Michele Borba. micheleborba.com
6 "National sexual assault rate highest since 1996, violent crimes up: Statistics Canada" by Marie-Danielle Smith, Canadian Press, August 3, 2022. In Canada the CBC published this article to support Dr. Borba's concern:
7 safewise.com/resources/internet-safety-for-teens

CHAPTER 30

Men and Boys

"Waste no more time arguing about what a good man should be. Be one."

MARCUS AURELIUS

Men and boys can end sexual exploitation. Every survivor has told me that men must stop exploiting and hurting women and girls. In 2016, a glaring example of sexual assault by a young man was the nineteen-year-old Stanford student and athlete Brock Turner[1] who sexually assaulted an unconscious young woman, Chanel Miller.

A person can be charged with sexual assault if they take advantage of someone who is drunk or high because a person who is drunk or high cannot give consent. The victim gave a sixteen-page impact statement that she read aloud in court and it went viral in international news. The public was outraged with the minimal sentence Turner received; three months served in jail. Meanwhile the victim lives with lifelong trauma. The victim has published her book on the experience.[2]

This is an opportunity for men to be the solution. Boys need to be raised to respect women and girls, and not treat them as objects. Men and boys need to take ownership and responsibility for their behaviour to counter unhealthy socialization. Boys need to be taught that girls have value and worth, and that every woman and girl has the right to be free of violence.

Men Stopping Violence[3] is an organization that for the past thirty-five years has provided a twenty-four-week program to all men interested in exploring the issue of violence against women. The questions they have men ask themselves:

- What am I doing?
- Why am I doing it?
- Is this hurtful or beneficial to another human being?
- What is true intimacy?
- Do I listen to another human being? Do I know how to listen?
- What does an equal sharing relationship look like?

Dr. Jennisue Jessen[4] is a survivor and member of the USA Advisory Council on Human Trafficking, established in 2015. Each member is a survivor and advises on federal anti-trafficking policies to the President's Interagency Task Force to Monitor and Combat Trafficking in Persons. In Dr. Jessen's powerful presentations, she describes being trafficked by her grandfather from age four to seventeen. She states, "We need men who are courageous in their masculinity. We need men who are co-equal, co-leaders to partner within our families. We need to teach men and boys their inherent worth and value. We need good strong Dads raising their children to be good strong people."

Survivors have told me that having a caring, concerned, protective and loving father would have kept them out of the sex industry.

"One good man, one good man,
it ain't much—it's only everything."

DEBORAH KERR

"A boy who is going to make a great man must not make up his mind merely to overcome a thousand obstacles, but to win in spite of a thousand repulses and defeats."

THEODORE ROOSEVELT

"The heart of a good man is the sanctuary of God in this world."

SUZANNE CURCHOD

"The first step to be a good man is this: you must deeply feel the burden of the stones someone else is carrying."

MEHMET MURAT ILDAN

"The true measure of a man is how he treats someone who can do him absolutely no good."

SAMUEL JOHNSON

Endnotes

1 "Brock Turner, ex-Stanford swimmer convicted of sex assault, loses bid for new trial" by Paul Elias, Associated Press, August 8, 2018.
2 "Chanel Miller is 'Emily Doe,' the woman at the centre of the Brock Turner Case"Associated Press, September 5, 2019.
   "Know My Name"by Chanel Miller, published by Viking, September 24, 2019.
3 menstoppingviolence.org
4 Dr. Jennisue Jessen, member of the U.S. Advisory Council on Human Trafficking. "Human Trafficking in Plain Sight: One in Five Children at Risk" by Pam Bales, North by Colorado Media Group, Jun/Jul 2022 Edition. This article is an introduction to Dr. Jessen and her work in counter-trafficking. compass31.com

Epilogue

Meaningful human connection is not measurable and cannot be seen, but it is what humanizes us. Dr. Mary Ann Layden states simply, "Love is the most important thing in the world."

This volume is a work in progress and an ongoing conversation. It is a brief introduction into the world of human trafficking, sexual exploitation and child sex trafficking.

The United States of America is decades ahead in public awareness work, public policy, law enforcement engagement and NGOs working on this issue. Canada has significant catch up to do to remain a Tier One country according to the Trafficking in Persons Report. For example, if the PCEPA Federal Law is repealed, Canada is at risk of losing the Tier One status. Globally this would send the message that Canada is open for sex tourism.

One person can make a difference in their sphere of influence, in their community, their country and ultimately in the world. It is easy to be depressed, disheartened and discouraged with such a dark issue. However, with the information in this book, the reader can be empowered to make a difference. The following Appendices provide a multitude of resources for any individual who wants to stop human trafficking, sexual exploitation, and child sex trafficking.

A modern equal civil society does not buy and sell women and children.

I am one person. Trying to make a difference. You can join me. You can make a difference, too.

"The responsibility to eliminate the sexual
exploitation of children through prostitution
rests with governments, parents, social and legal
organizations, law enforcement, the criminal-justice
system, and society as a whole. It is only with
combined efforts that the goal of dignified, valued,
and respected lives for all children, at home and
abroad, can be achieved."

NATIONAL CENTER FOR MISSING AND EXPLOITED CHILDREN, USA

Appendices

The Law

It is important to understand the Federal Law that is in place in Canada. The intent of the law is made clear in the Preamble to the Law. The goal is to protect communities and exploited persons.

Preamble to the Canadian Federal Law, "The Protection of Communities and Exploited Persons Act."

Whereas the Parliament of Canada has grave concerns about the exploitation that is inherent in prostitution and the risks of violence posed to those who engage in it;

Whereas the Parliament of Canada recognizes the social harm caused by the objectification of the human body and the commodification of sexual activity;

Whereas it is important to protect human dignity and the equality of all Canadians by discouraging prostitution, which has a disproportionate impact on women and children;

Whereas it is important to continue to denounce and prohibit the procurement of persons for the purpose of prostitution and the development of economic interests in the exploitation of the prostitution of others as well as the commercialization and institutionalization of prostitution;

Whereas the Parliament of Canada wishes to encourage those who engage in prostitution to report incidents of violence and to leave prostitution;

And whereas the Parliament of Canada is committed to protecting communities from the harms associated with prostitution;

Now, therefore, Her Majesty, by and with the advice and consent of the Senate and Hour of Commons of Canada, enacts as follows:

"The Protection of Communities and Exploited Persons Act."

My Brief to the Federal Justice Committee on PCEPA Review

Brief Submission for the Federal Justice Committee
February 13, 2022

TOPIC: PCEPA (Protection of Communities and Exploited Persons) Review

Submitted by:
Mrs. Cathy Peters
BC anti-human trafficking educator, speaker, advocate
Be Amazing Campaign; Stop Sexual Exploitation
beamazingcampaign.org

TITLE:
The importance of keeping and strengthening the "Protection of Communities and Exploited Persons Act" in Canada

QUESTIONS:
1. What is the strength of PCEPA? The FOCUS on discouraging the DEMAND and the buying of sex which addresses the ROOT CAUSE of prostitution, trafficking, sexual exploitation. The Preamble to the LAW is concise and gives the INTENT of the Law to stop the harms caused by prostitution.

2. Why is discouraging DEMAND KEY in addressing prostitution? "Discouraging The Demand" is the name of a 2021 OSCE report regarding human trafficking for the purposes of sexual exploitation. The motor behind this...is money, as global yearly profits are estimated at around 100 billion dollars. Canada has signed the Palermo Protocol and has a legal obligation to discourage DEMAND (Article 9, Section 5).

3. What has PCEPA accomplished so far? a) There is now discussion in Canada about the HARMS of prostitution. b) More Prevention Education organizations have developed; i.e. The National Human Trafficking Education Centre by the Joy Smith Foundation. c) Law Enforcement do not criminalize sellers of sex, but recognize the HARM they endure. d) The National Human Trafficking Hotline is set up under the Canadian Centre to End Human

Trafficking. They have submitted their first nation-wide report, which helps to understand the issue and provide data in Canada.

4. Are prostitution and trafficking linked? While not all prostituted persons are trafficked, trafficking is for the purpose of prostitution. They cannot be de-linked. The vast majority in the sex industry are trafficked or pimped. Page 4, The Nordic Model of Prostitution: A change in perspective in protection of human dignity" by Dr. Ingeborg Kraus, September 18, 2021. TRAUMA AND PROSTITUTION; Scientists for a World Without Prostitution.

5. What amendments are needed? a) The definition for human trafficking in Canada needs to follow the definition in the Palermo Protocol. The current definition in Canada includes the need for the victim to state FEAR, and this requirement of removing Fear as a factor needs to be removed. b) Funding and training for law enforcement needs to accompany the strengthening of PCEPA. c) The 3rd element of PCEPA is the provision of EXIT SERVICES for sellers of sex. Currently, monies are given to HARM REDUCTION agencies that inadvertently support the sex industry so it can continue to grow. Monies should NOT be given to organizations that support full decriminalization of prostitution, or that undermine anti-human trafficking efforts, because it contravenes PCEPA, the Federal Law. Monies should be given to vetted organizations that provide full wrap around programs such as Covenant House or Salvation Army (Deborah's Gate). NOTE: Has the National Action Plan to Combat Human Trafficking been followed?

6. What GAPS are not being addressed in Canada? Trafficking in Persons Report by the USA State Department cites these Gaps: a) comprehensive data is needed on investigations, prosecutions, convictions and victims services b) quality and timely delivery of trafficking-specific services are needed c) there needs to be coordination between federal and provincial governments on anti-trafficking measures d) there needs to be proactive law enforcement techniques, increased training for prosecutors and judges and increased partnerships with private sector to prevent human trafficking.

7. What are negative outcomes if PCEPA is repealed? Canada would become "America's brothel." Canada shares the longest border in the world with the USA, and there is only some counties in Nevada that have legalized prostitution. Americans would come to Canada to buy sex. Any country or community that allows prostitution attracts more prostitution and attracts sex

buyers. This has occurred in Germany, Netherlands, Thailand, Nevada and now New Zealand. Canada would become a global sex tourism destination.

8. Can there be a middle ground? There is no middle ground; Canada either supports gender equality and human rights OR prostitution. Both cannot exist together. Prostitution violates human dignity and prevents equality between men and women. For example, "On April 16, 2016, the French National Assembly passed a prohibition on sex-buying with the following reason: "Prostitution is physical, psychological and sexual violence, and affront to human dignity and in violation of the principle of equality between men and women." www.academia.edu/28982923/Das_franzoisische_Gesetz_zur_ Freierbestrafung by Dr. Inge Kleine (The French Law Punishing Sex Buyers).

9. Is the New Zealand Model working? New Zealand is cited as the Gold Standard by the sex industry. New Zealand is a very isolated country in the Pacific Ocean sharing no borders. Read the Trafficking in Persons Report 2021 and 2022 by the USA State Department to see that New Zealand has dropped to a Tier 2 country because of increased human trafficking and child sex trafficking. "The profiteers of the system of prostitution maintain a very large influence on many politicians, disseminating a romanticized view of prostitution…and who view prostitution as an occupation of choice…leading to the creation of legal frameworks that enable women's degradation as cheap products and their sexual exploitation." Page 2, "The Nordic Model of Prostitution: A change in perspective in protection of human dignity" by Dr. Ingeborg Kraus, September 18, 2021. TRAUMA AND PROSTITUTION; Scientists for a World Without Prostitution.

10. Does legalized or fully decriminalized prostitution increase Human Trafficking? The comparative study, "Does Legalized Prostitution Increase Human Trafficking?" investigated the sex trade in 150 countries with three independent researchers from Berlin, Heidelberg and London, concluding that a liberalized prostitution law, such as the one introduced by Germany in 2002, leads to an increase in human trafficking. The number of prostitutes in Germany is 60 times higher than Sweden, even though the Swedish population is just 10 times smaller. Page 8, "The Nordic Model of Prostitution: A change in perspective in protection of human dignity", by Dr. Ingeborg Kraus, TRAUMA AND PROSTITUTION, Scientists for a world without prostitution.

11. What is a recent case in Canada? R vs. Alcorn (2021 MBCA 101 Date:20211209) – In Manitoba an underage Indigenous girl was sexually exploited and committed suicide. The perpetrator requested a lesser sentence and the judges quadrupled the sentence. This is a precedent setting court case in Canada illustrating the targeted harm to Indigenous youth. Other cases: Robert Pickton, Highway of Tears, Reza Moazami.

12. What is the impact of prostitution on youth and children? Prostitution could not exist if UNDERAGE individuals were not recruited; the sex industry relies on underage recruitment. PCEPA 2014, "Sex Industry Slavery; Protecting Canada's Youth" by Dr. Robert Chrismas, University of Toronto Press, 2020, Joy Smith Foundation

13. What factors contribute to increased Human Sex Trafficking (for the purpose of prostitution)? Globalization, Unregulated Technology, Limited Law enforcement and Little Prevention Education. Valiant Richey, Special Representative and Co-ordinator for Combating Trafficking in Human Beings, OSCE, Organization for the Security and Cooperation in Europe, representing 57 countries and 1 billion people.

14. NOTE: There is no "consent" if there is no choice. There is no "consent" if there is coercion or manipulation. That leaves a very small number of individuals who choose to be prostituted.

15. How does Law Enforcement enforce PCEPA? Follow templates from cities that are using PCEPA and criminalizing johns. Templates can be from the USA, and Sweden. Having a simultaneous rollout Education campaign is necessary. In Sweden this is effective. Social Workers working in tandem with police is effective. School Liaison Officers in schools is a highly effective tool because recruiting is occurring in schools.

SOURCES

- Stats Canada, Juristat Canada
- RCMP Human Trafficking Coordination Centre
- Federal Public Safety Ministry: Human Trafficking Center
- OCTIP: Office to Combat Trafficking in Persons (BC)
- Children of the Street (PLEA): prevention education program in BC reaching over 25,000 youth in Grades 3–12
- SEE: Sexual Exploitation Education by Tiana Sharifi, owner, founder, educator
- TIP: Trafficking in Persons Reports by USA State Department (on Canada, New Zealand)
- Book, "Sex Industry Slavery: Protecting Canada's Youth" by Dr. Robert Chrismas, University of Toronto, 2020.
- Joy Smith Foundation
- NCOSE: National Center on Sexual Exploitation, Washington, DC
- Shared Hope International, Washington State, USA
- OSCE: Organization for the Security and Cooperation in Europe; largest security organization in the world representing 57 countries, 1 billion people. Report, "Discouraging DEMAND-that fosters trafficking for the purpose of sexual exploitation" by Valiant Richey, OSCE Special representative and Coordinator for Combating Trafficking in Human Beings.
- Report, "The Nordic Model of Prostitution: A change in perspective in protection of human dignity" by Dr. Ingeborg Kraus, July 2, 2021.
- Trauma and Prostitution: Scientists for a World Without Prostitution.
- VCASE.ca: Vancouver Collective Against Sexual Exploitation; excellent source of videos and research.
- BeAmazingCampaign.org: my website with educational handouts and resources

Human Trafficking Definitions Handout

Source: Shared Hope International

WHAT IS HUMAN TRAFFICKING?

Sex trafficking is a booming industry. Sex trafficking occurs when someone uses force, fraud or coercion to cause a commercial sex act with an adult or causes a minor to commit a commercial sex act. A commercial sex act includes prostitution, pornography and sexual performance done in exchange for any item of value, such as money, drugs, shelter, food or clothes. It thrives because there is serious demand.

Buyer: fuels the market with their money
Trafficker/pimp: exploits victims to earn revenue from buyers
Victim: includes both girls and boys who are bought and sold for profit

Traffickers find victims through social network, home/neighbourhood, clubs or bars, internet, school, and lure them though promises protection, love, adventure, home, opportunity.

TRAFFICKERS USE FEAR, VIOLENCE, INTIMIDATION, THREATS to ensure compliance and meet demand. The common age a child enters sex trafficking is thirteen years old (ten to twelve years of age in larger urban centres); too young and naïve to realize what's happening. Society may call it prostitution, but federal law calls it sex trafficking.

Because of social stigma or misinformation, victims go **unidentified** (silenced by fear and the control of the trafficker), **misidentified** (pigeonholed into treatment for only surface issues). So, sex trafficked children are instead treated for drug abuse, alcohol abuse, domestic violence, delinquency, teenage pregnancy, STIs, abortion... all masking the true need...

FREEDOM.

Solutions and Resources Handout

This is a simple, useful resource that helps parents and caregivers tackle the issue. I hand it out to politicians, police and the public when I make presentations in British Columbia.

Preventing Child Sex Trafficking in BC
Buying and selling children for sex is one of the fastest growing crimes in Canada, and it is happening in communities across BC.

Globalization, unregulated technology, lack of law enforcement, and inadequate prevention education is allowing this crime to grow globally.

Human sex trafficking (HT) involves the recruitment, transportation or harbouring of people for the purpose of exploitation through the use of force, coercion, fraud, deception or threats against the victim or person known to them. It is known as modern day slavery. According to the US State department's annual global report on trafficking in persons (TIP), Canada is a source, transit and destination for sex trafficking. state.gov/j/tip/rls/

Child sex trafficking is a lucrative crime. It has low costs and huge profits; a trafficker can make hundreds of thousands of dollars per victim, per year. The average age of entry into prostitution in Canada is twelve to fourteen years of age, although traffickers are known to target younger children. Traffickers seek young victims both to service the demand for sex with those who look young, and because these victims are easier to manipulate and control.

The biggest problem in Canada is that people do not know there is a problem; therefore, child sex trafficking is expanding in the dark. Every child can be a target and a potential victim but learning about this issue is the first step.

Five things that parents can do to help prevent their children from being lured into sex trafficking:

1. Set a high standard of love within your home
The way you define and express love shapes your children's self-image, confidence and opinions of future relationships. Treat them the way you

want their future partners to treat them. Help them to distinguish between real love and empty promises or cheap gifts.

2. Talk to your children about sexual abuse
According to the US Department of Justice, someone in the US is sexually assaulted every two minutes, of which 29% are between the ages of twelve and seventeen. Let your children know that if anyone has or ever does hurt them, they can talk to you. This is the most important thing you can say. Don't assume they have not been hurt by sexual violence before. Leave the door open for your child to talk about past circumstances that they haven't shared with you.

3. Talk to your children about sex trafficking
Discuss ways children and teens are targeted for sex trafficking. Let them know that traffickers specifically try to woo young girls and boys with promises of a better life, whether it's promises of love and attention, or promises of nice things and trips. Traffickers can be male or female, even classmates. Traffickers may even use youth to recruit other youth.

4. Talk to your children about the dangers of social media
It is important to provide practical safety tips, such as: don't share personal information on the internet; don't accept Facebook requests from unknown people; never share naked photos of yourself with anyone; and tell a parent or a trusted adult if you feel threatened or uncomfortable online. Children also need help defining friendships. Teach them that a friend is not someone you met yesterday and that a "friend" on Facebook is not the same thing as a friendship.

5. Pay attention to your children
Monitor your children's social media accounts. Look for ways to meet their friends, their friends' parents and those they hang out with. Be alert to boyfriends who are much older, or friendships that tend to isolate your child from other friends or family. Take notice if your child has new clothing items, makeup products, cell phone or other items and ask how they acquired them.

RESOURCES AND LINKS
- Covenant House: Crises program for ages 16–24
  info@covenanthousebc.org / 604-685-7474
- Kids Help Phone: 1-800-668-6868
- Fraser Health Forensic Nurse Service: Surrey Memorial Hospital
  604-953-4723

- Internet Safety Tips: cybertip.ca
- Office to Combat Trafficking in Persons (OCTIP): 1-888-712-7974 604-660-5199 / octip@gov.bc.ca
- Plea Community Services Society assisting youth 24/7: onyx@plea.bc.ca / 604-708-2647
- Vancouver Rape Relief and Women's Shelter (24/7): 604-872-8212 / info@rapereliefshelter.bc.ca
- Trafficking Resource Centre (USA): Polaris Project USA National Human Trafficking Hotline: 1-888-373-7888 / traffickingresourcecenter.org
- VictimLink BC (24/7): 1-800-563-0808
- Youth Against Violence (24/7): info@youthagainstviolenceline.com 1-800-680-4264

AUTHORITIES CONTACTS
- RCMP: For help and to report to police, call 911 / rcmp-grc.gc.ca
- Ministry of Child Protection Services: 1-800-663-9122 / 604-660-4927 (24 hours) or if a child is in danger, to reach Ministry of Child and Family Development: 604-310-1234
- Crime Stoppers: 1-800-222-TIPS (8477)
- National Human Trafficking Hotline Number: 1-833-900-1010

ADDITIONAL RESOURCES
Children of the Street Society in Coquitlam provides prevention education in B.C. schools, addressing 25,000 students in a school year from grades three through twelve. They have an excellent website with tools and resources listed for every community in B.C.
childrenofthestreet.com

Joy Smith Foundation (Manitoba) provides prevention education, resources and an overview of human sex trafficking Canada.
joysmithfoundation.com

Shared Hope International (Washington State) sponsors The JuST (Juvenile Sex Trafficking) Conference in the USA, an event that spotlights the most pressing issues in the anti-trafficking field.
justconference.org

Strategies for Civic Governments

Civic Governments want strategies to address Human Sex Trafficking and Sexual Exploitation. Below are eight simple strategies that can be implemented.

Learn about the issue at beamazingcampaign.org, read "Invisible Chains" by Benjamin Perrin (UBC Law professor), follow Human trafficking expert in Canada former Manitoba MP Joy Smith at joysmithfoundation.com. Have staff take the BC OCTIP (Office to Combat Trafficking in Persons) free online course. Encourage police to take HT course on the Police Knowledge Network.

Incorporate the United Nations Four Pillars in a local strategy to stop Human trafficking/sexual exploitation: Prevention, Protection, Prosecution, Partnerships.

Prevention: raise awareness in community. Children of the Street (Plea) does school and community programs. Encourage "Men End Exploitation" movements: Moosehide Campaign, Westcoast Boys Club Network. Support porn addiction services for youth; "Fightthenewdrug" program recognizing the public health effects to youth of viewing violent sexual material. Use communications to raise awareness: Calgary has "Not in My City" campaign, Ontario has "Saving the girl next door program", the RCMP has the "I'm Not for Sale" campaign. Sports events- Manitoba, Grey Cup "Sex is not a sport" campaign. King County (Seattle) has "Buyer Beware" program.

Protection: help victims, have exit strategies in place for them, consider 24/7 "wrap-around programs" Salvation Army "Deborah's Gate", Covenant House, Servants Anonymous, Union Gospel Mission.

Prosecution: increase policing budget, training and priorities. Have "buyer" deterrents in place, enforce the law; "Protection of Communities and Exploited Persons Act" which criminalizes "demand"- the profiteers, facilitators, buyers of commercially paid sex.

Partnerships: Train community stakeholders: Health care workers, fire department, municipal business licensing managers, educators, businesses to recognize human trafficking/sexual exploitation. Fraser Health Authority has a human trafficking protocol, Surrey Fire department is trained to recognize HT indicators. Train judges/Crown Counsel/criminal justice system.

Collaboration: with other cities and municipalities at local government associations, Police agencies and RCMP, three levels of government (civic, provincial, federal); UBCM, FCM with Resolutions.

Goal: safe, healthy, vibrant communities that are fit for families, youth, children and all vulnerable populations. Do not accept or support the full decriminalization of prostitution because the vulnerable (Indigenous women and girls, new migrants) in our communities are the most targeted, being lured, groomed and exploited for the sex industry.

National Human Trafficking Hotline Number: 1-833-900-1010

Strategies for Law Enforcement

Law enforcement needs basic protocol and strategies to deter sexual exploitation. Here are Five Strategies for Police:

1. Awareness
All Police need to be aware of the issue and know the law. Take HT training courses (Police Knowledge Network, OCTIP; Office to Combat Training In Persons). Read "Invisible Chains" by UBC law professor, Benjamin Perrin. Google: beamazingcampaign.org for a resource. Incorporate the United Nations 4 Pillars in a local strategy to combat trafficking: Prevention, Protection, Prosecution, Partnerships.

2. Address Demand
Until there is a deterrent for demand, this crime will increase. Johns, the buyers of sex, facilitators, profiteers need to be targeted and charged; this is the Federal law (Protection of Communities and Exploited Persons Act).

3. School Liaison Officer Program
Develop positive and strong liaisons with elementary and high school students. Young people are vulnerable and are being targeted. "Education is our greatest weapon." Digital safety training is needed for youth/parents.

4. Inventory Scan
Assess your community. Look for sex ads (Backpage, Craigslist, the newspaper, Georgia Strait); these will lead you to the buyers and sellers. List the businesses that are endemic to HT: escort services, modeling agencies, casinos, adult entertainment centers, tattoo parlours, holistic health centers, nail spas, day spas, unregistered massage parlours, strip clubs, cheap hotels and bars. Be aware of their services/clientele. List all your community resources to support victims.

5. Best Practices
Valiant Richey is the OSCE, the Organization for Security and Co-operation in Europe: Special Representative and Co-ordinator for Combating trafficking in Human Beings for 57 nation states with 1 billion people. Sweden has successfully implemented and funded the Nordic Model of Law for the past 22 years: contact Detective Inspector Simon Haggstrom, head of

the Stockholm Police Prostitution Unit (his work is to charge johns). USA-Demand.org has a list of police agencies addressing this crime. Washington State with former Congresswoman Linda Smith and NGO "Shared Hope"; Seattle, King County. Dallas Police Department, Houston City Council have extensive trainings in sexual exploitation/human trafficking. In Canada: Halifax police, RCMP operated "Northern Spotlight Operations." London, Ontario and London Women's Abuse Center work with law enforcement, Montreal vice unit, Peel Region Police in Hamilton, Winnipeg police and former MP Joy Smith, who introduced Human trafficking laws in Canada, with the Joy Smith Foundation and the Tracia Trust in Manitoba, York police in Toronto with survivor Casandra Diamond of Bridge North, Ontario has a strategic plan with a Human Trafficking Coordinator.

Resources

This is a list of the books, videos and research I have found particularly helpful.

BOOKS
1. "Somebody's Daughter" by Phonse Jessome, 1996, Nimbus Publishing. ISBN 1-55109-174-7. Pimping in Canada and its beginnings; the Toronto/Halifax pimping ring.
2. "Prostitution, Trafficking, and Traumatic Stress" by Melissa Farley, 2003, Routledge. ISBN 0-7890-2378-4.
3. "Invisible Chains" by UBC Law Professor Benjamin Perrin, 2010 Viking Canada. ISBN 978-0-670-06453-3. A must-read textbook on sex trafficking in Canada.
4. "Half the Sky" by Nicholas Kristof, 2010 Vintage Books. ISBN 978-0-307-38709-7. Good overview of the global sex trade. Excellent primer to the issue.
5. "Pornland" by Dr. Gail Dines, 2010, Beacon. ISBN 978-0870-0154-7. The impact of pornography on our culture by porn research expert. View Dr. Dines TED Talk.
6. "Girls Like Us" by Rachel Lloyd, 2011, Harper Perennial. ISBN 978-0-06-158206-6. Human sex trafficking in USA.
7. "Renting Lacy: A Story of America's Prostituted Children" by former Washington State Congresswoman Linda Smith, 2013, Shared Hope International.
8. "Paid For: My Journey Through Prostitution" by Rachel Moran, 2013, W. W. Norton & Co. ISBN 978-0-393-35197-2. A thorough treatise on what prostitution really looks by a survivor in Ireland.
9. "Walking Prey" by Holly Austin Smith, 2014, St. Martin's Press. ISBN 978-1-137-27873-9. Gives strategies to end exploitation at the back of the book.
10. "Made in the USA: The Sex Trafficking of America's Children" by Alisa Jordheim, 2014, HigherLife Publishing and Marketing. ISBN 978-1-939183-40-8.
11. "That Lonely Section of Hell" by Lorimer Shenher, 2015, Greystone Books. ISBN 978-1-77164-257-6. The Robert Pickton investigation.
12. "Shadow's Law" by Swedish Detective Inspector Simon Haggstrom, 2016, Bullet Point Publishing. ISBN 978-91-88153-20-3. The true story of an officer fighting prostitution.

13. "Victim Law: The Law of Victims of Crime in Canada" by Benjamin Perrin, 2017, Thomson Reuters. ISBN 978-0-7798-7766-9. The new field of law addressing the rights of victims in the justice system.
14. "The True Story of Canadian Human Trafficking" by Paul H. Boge, 2018, Castle Quay Books. ISBN 978-1988-9280-98. The true story of human trafficking in Canada from the perspective of the Manitoba MP Joy Smith who did something to try and stop it.
15. "Not a Choice, Not a Job" by Dr. Janice G. Raymond, 2019, Potomac Books. ISBN 978-1-61234-626-7. Exposing the myths about prostitution and the global sex trade.
16. "Sex Industry Slavery: Protecting Canada's Youth" by Dr. Robert Chrismas, 2020, University of Toronto Press. ISBN 978-1-4875-2485-2. A police officer's perspective into Canada's sex industry.

VIDEOS
1. "Amy's Story: Covenant House Toronto" youtube.com/watch?v=vb3os7i9gB4
2. "Kailey Heywood's Love Story" (UK Police)
3. PSA from Joy Smith Foundation (40 seconds)
4. Trailer from "Red Light Green Light" documentary by Jared and Michelle Brock; a three-minute overview of the global problem.
5. "Trisha Baptie TED Talk" DTE survivor. (15 minutes)
6. "We are the Lions" spoken word cinema by YWCA Tennessee.
7. "Break the Silence" Canadian version music video from three Canadian girls who were trafficked.
8. Public Safety Canada: Human Trafficking PSA
9. "Nameless: A Documentary about Child Sex Trafficking" by MSCR (Men Can Stop Rape), Washington, DC. This is an American production that emphasizes the key principles I describe in this book. The difference in Canada is that we have the partial decriminalization law or Equality Model called the Protection of Communities and Exploited Persons Act that criminalizes the demand. The root cause of the harm is the buyer of sex, and this is recognized in Canadian Law.

RESEARCH ARTICLES
Demand reduction strategies
A National Overview of Prostitution and Sex Trafficking Demand Reduction Efforts Final Report Grant #2008-IJ-CX-0010 April 30, 2012. Prepared for the National Institute of Justice Office of Justice Programs, USA Department of Justice 810 Seventh Street, NW Washington, D.C. 20531. Submitted by

Michael Shively, Ph.D. Kristina Kliorys, Kristin Wheeler, Dana Hunt, Ph.D. Abt Associates Inc. 55 Wheeler St. Cambridge, MA 02138. This document is a research report submitted to the USA Department of Justice. This report has not been published by the Department. Opinions or points of view expressed are those of the author(s) and do not necessarily reflect the official position or policies of the USA Department of Justice.

Detailed summary about Canada's Tier One efforts
Trafficking in Persons Report 2022 from the USA State Department. Every year there is a summary of what is being done in every country globally. While Canada is listed as Tier One, it meets minimal standards only. Data collection lacks, as does consistent law enforcement. Prevention education and public awareness is limited.

On demand
"Best practices to Address the Demand Side of Sex Trafficking" by Dr. Donna M. Hughes, Professor, and Eleanor M. and Oscar M. Carlson. Endowed Chair Women's Studies Program, University of Rhode Island, August 2004. Cooperative Agreement Number S-INLEC-04-CA-0003.

Overview on demand
In-depth report to examine commercial sex markets with the purpose of addressing demand. The biography list in this report is extensive and I found more articles from this source. "Demand. A Comparative Examination of Sex Tourism and Trafficking in Jamaica, Japan, the Netherlands and the United States" by Shared Hope International, funded by the Office to Monitor and Combat Trafficking in Persons, US Department of State.

Article on the impact of full decriminalization of prostitution in the state of Rhode Island for 29 years:
"Decriminalized Prostitution: Impunity for Violence and Exploitation" by Melanie Shapiro, Esq. and Donna M. Hughes, Ph.D. This detailed research describes the impact of full decriminalization in Rhode Island for twenty-nine years until the state government repealed the law.

Dr. Donna Hughes was instrumental in repealing the law in Rhode Island after 29 years of full decriminalization:
"Best Practices to Address the Demand Side of Sex Trafficking" by Donna M. Hughes, Professor, Women's Studies Program, University of Rhode Island, August 2004.

Prostitution and sex trafficking link

"The Links Between Prostitution and Sex Trafficking: A Briefing Handbook" by Monica O'Connor and Grainne Healy, Joint Project Coordinated by the Coalition Against Trafficking in Women (CATW) and the European Women's Lobby (EWL) on Promoting Preventative Measures to Combat Trafficking in Human Beings for Sexual Exploitation: A Swedish and United States Governmental and Non-Governmental Organisation Partnership, 2006.

Manifesto, Joint CATW-EWL Press Conference, 2005: "We, the survivors of prostitution and trafficking gathered at his press conference today, declare that prostitution is violence against women. Women in prostitution do not wake up one and "choose" to be prostitutes. It is chosen for us by poverty, past sexual abuse, the pimps who take advantage of our vulnerabilities and the men who buy us for the sex of prostitution."

The author's contribution to a report

"Moving Forward in the Fight Against Human Trafficking In Canada: Report of the Standing Committee on Justice and Human Rights"by Chair Anthony Housefather. December 2018, 42nd Parliament, 1st Session. Many organizations contributed to this report.

Review on Indigenous women and girls

"Sexual Exploitation and Trafficking of Aboriginal Women and Girls: A Literature Review and Key Informant Interviews." Report prepared by Native Women's Association of Canada, March 2014, commissioned by the Canadian Women's Foundation.

Report on Canada

"No More: Ending Sex Trafficking In Canada; Report of the National Task Force on Sex Trafficking of Women and Girls in Canada." Commissioned by the Canadian Women's Foundation, Fall 2014. This is their best report. After 2014 the Canadian Women's Foundation took a harm reduction approach rather than supporting a gender equality/human rights approach.

Article on Indigenous and local

"Prostitution in Vancouver: Violence and Colonization of First Nations Women" by Melissa Farley, Jacqueline Lynne, Ann Cotton, Transcultural Psychiatry, June 2005. One of the few research articles that is Vancouver focused.
Vol. 42 (2) 242-271 DOI: 10.1177/1363461505052667

Human trafficking trends in Canada
The Canadian Centre to End Human Trafficking, 2019–2020.
canadiancentretoendhumantrafficking.ca

Prostitution research education website by global researcher Dr. Melissa Farley
"Prostitution and Trafficking in Nine Countries" by eight authors including Melissa Farley, article in Journal of Trauma Practice, January 2004, from Prostitution Research and Education, San Francisco CA, USA.

Does legalization increase human trafficking?
2012 study of 150 countries, published in journal "World Development" by Seo-Young Cho, Axel Dreher, Eric Neumayer. On average, countries where prostitution is legal, experience larger reported Human Trafficking inflows.

"Online Prostitution and Trafficking"
By Melissa Farley Ph.D., Kenneth Franzblau J.D., and M. Alexis Kennedy J.D., Ph.D, 2014. Statistics and research.
humantraffickingresearch.org/resource/online-prostitution-and-trafficking/

Canadians support current PCEPA Law
"Canadians are five times more likely to support than oppose Canada's current prostitution legislation" Conducted by NANOS for London Abused Women's Centre, July 2020.

Article for British Columbia
"Commercial Sexual Exploitation of Children and Youth" Issue BCMJ, Vol. 46, No. 3, April 2004. Pages 119–122 Clinical articles by Marie D. Hay, MD, DCH, DRCOG, FRCPC, MRCP (UK), pediatrician from Prince George. One of the few research articles that is B.C. focused.

Reducing male demand
"Of Vice and Men: A New Approach to Eradicating Sex Trafficking by Reducing Male Demand Through Educational Programs and Abolitionist Legislation" by Iris Yen, Journal of Criminal Law and Criminology, Volume 98, Issue 2 Winter, Article 6.

Demand abolition: the evidence against legalizing prostitution
Thorough presentation and arguments for abolition by Ian Kitterman.
ian_kitterman@huntalternatives.org

"10 Reasons for Not Legalizing Prostitution"
A summary against legalization by global expert researcher by Dr. Janice G. Raymond (CATW, 2003)

Canada
"Taking Action To End Violence Against Young Women And Girls In Canada: Report of the Standing Committee on the Status of Women" by Marilyn Gladu, Chair, March 2017, 42nd Parliament, 1st Session.

Research on children
Pediatrics, Official Journal of the American Academy of Pediatrics, "The Evaluation of Children in the Primary Care Setting When Sexual Abuse is Suspected" by Carole Jenny, James E. Crawford-Jakubiak and Committee on Child Abuse and Neglect, July 29, 2013. DOI: 10.1542/peds.2013-1741 pediatrics.aapublications.org/content/early/2013/07/23/peds.2013-1741
The American Academy of Pediatrics is dedicated to the health of all children.

Child sex tourism
"US Domestic Prosecution of the American International Sex Tourist: Efforts to Protect Children from Sexual Exploitation" by Sara K. Andrews, Journal of Criminal Law and Criminology, Volume 94, Issue 2 Winter, Article 6.

Canada
"An Assessment of Sex Trafficking" by Nicole A. Barrett, Director, Global Justice Associates, May 2013, commissioned by Canadian Women's Foundation; a Task Force on Trafficking of Women and Girls in Canada.

A feminist speaks up
"Everybody's Doing It! And Other Bad Arguments in Defense of Prostitution" by Meghan Murphy, December 9, 2016.
feministcurrent.com/author/megmin/

Canada and the Federal Law
"Debra M. Haak: Canada's Laws designed to deter prostitution, not keep sex workers safe" by Debra Haak, December 21, 2018. vancouversun.com/author/debra-haak

RCMP Reports
RCMP Human Trafficking National Coordination Centre: 2015 Statistics on Human Trafficking. RCMP Human Trafficking National Coordination Centre: 2013 report on Domestic Human trafficking for Sexual Exploitation in Canada.

Stats Canada Reports
"Trafficking in Persons in Canada, 2014" by Maisie Karam, Canadian Centre for Justice Statistics, July 12, 2016.

Canadian statistics
"Prostitution Offences in Canada: Statistical Trends" by Cristine Rotenberg, Canadian Centre for Justice Statistics, November 10, 2016.

Timely journalism
"Missing and Murdered: The Trafficked" by Tavia Grant, Globe and Mail, February 10, 2016. "Unfounded: Police Dismiss 1 in 5 Sexual Assaults Claims as Baseless" by Robyn Doolittle, Globe and Mail, February 3, 2017. theglobeandmail.com

Best overview globally of men and women involved in the sex industry
"The John's" and "The Natasha's" by Victor Malarek, award-winning Canadian journalist who has done one of the few books covering John research. Page 246 Malarek states, "...the root cause of prostitution is that men buy."

National Action Plan to Combat Human Trafficking
2014–2015 Annual Report on Progress, Public Safety Canada

Doctoral dissertation by former police officer
"Modern Day Slavery and the Sex Industry: Raising the Voices of Survivors and Collaborators While Confronting Sex Trafficking and Exploitation in Manitoba, Canada" Doctoral Thesis by Robert W. Chrismas (former Winnipeg Police Officer), Faculty of Peace and Conflict Studies University of Manitoba, Winnipeg, 2017. Quote from Manitoba Attorney General Andrew Swan, "We have a new Criminal Code provision (PCEPA) in Canada which for the first time in our country's history, have made it illegal to buy sex, full stop. With these new laws we can open the door to focus on the demand-side."

Main issues in prostitution
This is an FAQ that addresses the main issues of prostitution.
Genderberg.com

Canadian Centre for the Protection of Children, Manitoba (Best Practices) and collaboration with cybertip.ca
"Child Sexual Abuse Images on the Internet": A Cybertip.ca Analysis, Cybertip.ca, January 2016, Canadian Centre for Child Protection.

Homeless youth
"Labour and Sex Trafficking Among Homeless Youth: A Ten-City Study Executive Summary", by Loyola University, New Orleans, 2014-2016. A Modern Slavery Research Project. This study provides a detailed account of labour and sexual exploitation experienced by homeless youth in Covenant House's Care in ten cities.

Canada
"Brief submitted to the House of Commons Standing Committee on Justice and Human Rights": National consultation on Human Trafficking in Canada, submitted by the Canadian Federation of University women, June 15, 2018.

Pornography and violent sexual images online in canada
"Motion M-47- Briefing Kit on Online Sexual Violence" by MP Arnold Viersen (Peace River- Westlock).

Background before the PCEPA
"Connecting the Dots: A Proposal for a National Action Plan to Combat Human Trafficking" by Joy Smith, B.Ed., M.Ed., former Member of Parliament Kildonan-St. Paul, Manitoba, 2011.

Article on demand
"The Problem of Demand in Combating Sex Trafficking" by Linda Smith and Samantha Healy Vardaman, Carin. Info, 2010/3 vol.81, pages 607–624.

British Columbia
B.C.'s Action Plan to Combat Human Trafficking, published March 2013, British Columbia Ministry of Justice. 2013–2016. (This Action Plan has not been reinstated since 2016).

Stats and bibliography/sources
"Policy report for Parliamentarians- Prostitution", ARPA Canada- Association for Reformed Political Action. Fall 2016. info@arpacanada.ca

One of the few articles on CST
"Child Sex Trafficking-Recognition, Intervention, and Referral: an Educational Framework to Guide Health Care Provider Practice" by Cathy L. Miller, University of Texas at Tyler, School of Nursing, Fall 1-8-2015.

Children of the Street Society in B.C.
"Sexual Exploitation and Trafficking of Children and Youth in Canada: A Prevention and Early Intervention Toolkit for Parents and Toolkit for Service Providers", Children of the Street Society

First human trafficking case in British Columbia
and longest sentence in Canada
Regina v. Moazami, 2014 BCSC 1727 (CanLII), 2014-09-15, Docket: 26108, in the Supreme Court of British Columbia: Reasons for Judgement by the Honorable Madam Justice Bruce. Counsel for the Crown: Damienne F. Darby and Kristin Bryson. This is the first human trafficking conviction in BC, 2014.

Canada best practices for health protocols for identifying human sex trafficking
Forensic Nursing training videos from Fraser Health Authority. victimsweek.gc.ca/stories-experience/video/fns.html. The online training and information about this program can be found at fraserhealth.ca/forensicnursing This is one of the best programs in the country.

Free training available on human trafficking in Canada: OCTIP
Office to Combat Training In Persons training video: Canada is Not Immune. A training video for politicians, police and the public.
www2.gov.bc.ca/gov/content/justice/criminal-justice/victims-of-crime/human-trafficking/human-trafficking-training

Shared Hope report cards on child and youth sex trafficking in the USA
Shared Hope International: Institute for Justice and Advocacy, 2021 Toolkit. reportcards.sharedhope.org

Index

CPSIA information can be obtained
at www.ICGtesting.com
Printed in the USA
LVHW072323190723
752844LV00026B/1511